WOULD YOU WORK
FOR YOU?

SAM GEIST

ADDINGTON &
WENTWORTH
INC.

TORONTO, ONTARIO
CANADA

NAPLES, FLORIDA
UNITED STATES

Published simultaneously in Canada and in the United States
by Addington & Wentworth, Inc.

For information address:

Addington & Wentworth, Inc.
327 Renfrew Drive, Suite 301
Markham, ON   CANADA L3R 9S8
(905) 475-1022

First Edition
First Printing

Library of Congress Control Number: 00-136163

Canadian Cataloguing in Publication Data:

Geist, Sam, 1945-

"WOULD YOU WORK FOR YOU?": Thought-provoking approaches to assist leaders better themselves, their relationships, their skills, their people and ultimately greatly better their organizations

Includes index.

ISBN 1-896984-12-6

1. Leadership   2. Management I Title

HD57.7.G43 2001   658.4'092   C00-901662-7

DEDICATION

To leaders everywhere who look in the mirror every morning,
see themselves where they want to be and work all day to get
a little closer.

ACKNOWLEDGMENTS

My deepest appreciation to respondents of my leadership survey for their words of wisdom—Henry Veenema, Ross Lederer, Bernie Brill, Jack Bingleman, Arthur Moll, R.F. Conlin, Sandy Kennedy, Michael Martino, Paul Pieschel, Kim Struble, Grace Cerniuk, Chris Davis, Pierre Nadeau, Mark Towe, Otto Papasadero, John Eccleston, Paul Hetherington, Randy Hooper, Adele Stevens, Peter Bracken, Dennis Watson, Lorne Campbell, Larry Marsh, Doug Raymond, Larry Quinlivan, Tom McNown, Keith Talbot, Terry J. Ruffell.

Once again my thanks to Michelle Avoledo for her unwavering encouragement as well as her tireless effort to input, proof and correct the text.

To all manuscript readers who generously gave of their time and offered most helpful insights, suggestions and criticism—Michael Geist, Fraser McAllan, Charlie Crockett, John Eccleston, Jacobo Schatz and Sara Geist.

To Terry Kounelas for his outstanding efforts and all his creative and his formatting talents.

To Steven Beattie for his precise editing and his conscientious attention to this project.

To my children Michael, Allison, Aaron, Sara, Rebecca, Jacobo and Josh for their love, continued support and interest.

And finally to my wife Rene for her invaluable assistance and ongoing support. Life would have been boring without her.

TABLE OF CONTENTS

PREFACE

Why another book on leadership in a marketplace overcrowded with materials discussing the subject? The answer is a simple one: despite the proliferation of books, tapes and seminars devoted to the topic, many of us are still struggling to become more effective leaders of ourselves and others in today's fast moving work environment. The rules have changed; the demands and needs of the workplace have changed. We must get a handle on the new rules; we must become well acquainted with the new demands and needs. We must reinvent ourselves. We must renew our ability to lead.

This book is not intended as a theoretical treatise for the CEOs of massive organizations. Rather, it is meant to be a hands-on guide to assist managers of neighborhood supermarkets become more aware of the specific factors that impinge on their specific environment, and to help supervisors of local McDonalds' better understand their employees. It is for leaders of SMEs (small, medium and entrepreneurial organizations), for retailers, manufacturers and distributors and for directors and team leaders of organizations and associations. It is for all those who want to do a better job tomorrow than they are doing today—for those who are interested in moving themselves, their people and their enterprises forward to be where the action is.

Why the title *Would You Work for You?* There's a short tale behind its choice. As a speaker, I'm always looking for new ideas, new stories, new examples to illustrate the points I make. A good friend, Keith Van Beek, former President of Toys R Us, Canada, called one day, very excited because he had thought of a great question to add to my arsenal. It went like this: "If you were unemployed and looking for a job today, would the people who work for you now—hire you?" I loved it, but found it a little too long and cumbersome, so I shortened it to, "Would you work for you?"

I use it all the time, and the reaction is always the same. Audiences look puzzled for a moment, slowly begin to smile, but in mid-smile their expressions change to rue. They become a little uncomfortable as they realize the answer is not as pleasant as they had hoped. Well, *would you work for you?* Not a simple decision, but one that you will be able to address more easily after you have finished this book.

In the course of my travels I speak to many people—from different organizations, industries and associations across much of the world. I also conduct internal re-evaluations to assist organizations operate more efficiently and effectively. My work affords me the opportunity to really talk to leaders, be they from large corporations or from small family run businesses—about what they feel a leader's role is, what they think leadership is all about.

What surprised me about their responses is that almost everyone—from leaders of large corporations to self-employed entrepreneurs—share the same aspirations, desires and needs. They want to succeed, to do well. Many feel they are doing satisfactorily, but they can do better. When they look at themselves in the mirror they are just a little uncomfortable at what they see. The truly impressive leaders—whether they are leaders of thousands, dozens, several or of themselves alone—realize that the need to improve is ever present. These leaders wear no blinkers. They realize there is no finished—no completed—no "we're just perfect the way we are." They are always on the lookout for the opportunity to make their organizations a little better. They exemplify the difference between the boss who says, "*Go—Do,*" and the leader who says, *"Let's Go. Let's Do."*

My many discussions with leaders and their followers, my years of experience, my listening to their stories and asking questions has resulted in *Would You Work for You?* This book is intended to share their insights, to highlight their ideas and to outline the strategies they use to encourage people to work for them, *happily*. It seeks to provide you, the reader, with opportunities to look at your own situation from a different perspective, to help you "see" something

"The boss drives his men; the leader coaches them. The boss depends upon authority; the leader on goodwill. The boss inspires fear; the leader inspires enthusiasm. The boss says: 'I'; the leader says 'WE.' The boss says: 'Get here on time;' the leader gets there ahead of time. The boss fixes the blame for the breakdown; the leader fixes the breakdown. The boss knows how it's done; the leader shows how. The boss says: 'GO;' the leader says, 'Let's GO!'"

H. GORDON SELFRIDGE, FOUNDER
SELFRIDGE'S DEPARTMENT STORE, LONDON, ENGLAND

you've never before seen, and to provide you with the tools to implement innovative leadership strategies you might never have considered. This book definitely encourages you do the "mirror test," no matter how uncomfortable that might be. Look at yourself in the mirror and ask yourself honestly: would you work for you? Would anyone else work for you? With the battle for talent raging, a positive response is vital to long term business survival. Loyalty can no longer be taken for granted; people are now much less hesitant to defect if they feel unhappy with their situation. Ask yourself if the people who work for you get up each morning, look in *their* mirrors and smile about coming to work. There are organizations with leaders who really do inspire that kind of response!

I recently considered my own leadership ability and decided that yes, I'd work for me, if only I met a few conditions. I'd work for me, if only it were:

- **less stressful**

- **more interesting**

- **a learning experience, a growing experience**

- **ego-gratifying**

- **fun to go to work**

- **more profitable and more rewarding**

I'm certain you too could come up with a list of conditions under which you'd be happy working for you. That's exactly what this book helps you to achieve. It helps you become the leader you want to work for. The book is divided into six chapters, each of which focuses on mastering one area to assist you reaffirm that you would, indeed, be happy to work for you.

Chapter One—*The Essence of Leadership* This chapter defines a leader and outlines the characteristics often associated with an outstanding leader. This section highlights various definitions of what is needed to be an effective leader, offered up by leaders of many and leaders of one.

Chapter Two—*Mirror Mirror on the Wall* To be the kind of leader you would want to work for, that is to be a leader who inspires others, you need to know yourself. You need to know who you are and what your goals are. This section offers suggestions for how to maximize your strengths—your positive leadership skills—and how to minimize your weaknesses. It outlines techniques to develop yourself, motivate yourself, decrease stress and increase self-discipline.

Chapter Three—*Up Close and Personal* Once you know yourself, you need to know your staff—the people you are leading. Many leaders think of their staff according to the function they perform for the company. But to get the most from your people you also need to think of them in terms of their wants, their needs and their aspirations. This section highlights strategies to make your organization a good place to work. It outlines suggestions to enhance your staff's skills to further create a positive environment in which people will want to work.

Chapter Four—Taking Care of Business Leaders need specific talents to do their jobs well. This section examines six highly rated capabilities of a good leader: hiring, team building, managing time, delegating, resolving conflict and decision making. Specific suggestions about how to improve in these areas as well as valuable insights for leaders of many or few, are provided.

Chapter Five—Making Connections One of my favorite areas of leadership is communication—it is absolutely vital for every leader. This section addresses the components of effective communication, gives examples to assist you apply these skills to situations of your own, and describes in detail techniques for becoming a better communicator. Since effective communication skills are needed at all times and in all situations—these particular ideas can be applied to family life as well as to business life.

Chapter Six—Moving Forward Once you've got your business humming successfully, how do you keep it moving? This section outlines strategies to keep your organization on the leading edge by ensuring that your leadership vision remains at the forefront and stays fresh, believable and attainable.

By its conclusion, *Would You Work for You?* will have given you novel options to consider, applicable ideas to implement and innovative directions in which to grow. It will enhance your leadership skills in the workplace and in the home. It will make you a better leader. It will make you a better person.

Chapter 1

The Essence of Leadership

What is the definition of a leader? After speaking to a great many leaders of both small and large businesses, I have come to the realization that there isn't ONE single definition.

DEFINING LEADERSHIP

Harry S. Truman defined a leader as someone "who can persuade people to do what they don't want to do, or what they're too lazy to do, and like it." Henry Veneema said that a leader is "the individual who everyone refers to as the leader, without the business card to prove it." George Fisher defines leadership as the ability to take "a group of people in a new direction or to higher levels of performance than they would have achieved without you." There seems to be as many definitions of leaders as there are people offering them.

As part of the research I conducted for this book, I distributed questionnaires to leaders asking what qualities they felt were integral to leadership. The following ten qualities were most often given.

- ◆ *able to inspire; to motivate*—provides inspirational leadership to get the organization and the people who work in it, moving—gladly.

- ◆ *excellent communicator*—makes connections, develops a network through which both the hard facts and the personal interest in the information reaches all participants—and returns back to the communicator, still intact.

♦ *of sound judgment*—uses one's own good sense and that of one's trusted advisers, to make courageous decisions.

♦ *of exemplary character*—be "mirror-testworthy;" looks at oneself and is satisfied with the image that looks back.

♦ *a visionary*—sees what no one else has yet dreamed and shares it so clearly that all who come in contact with the vision believe in it as well.

♦ *"what-it-takes" intelligence*—thinks on many different levels simultaneously.

♦ *outstanding people skills*—demonstrates a great sensitivity to the needs of their people.

♦ *is passionate*—lights up and moves the organization with enthusiasm.

♦ *is compassionate*—demonstrates empathy and understanding for associates and staff alike.

♦ *executes consistently*—marshals oneself, all one's resources and organizes staff to take action.

"An outstanding leader is a person who knows where he wants the organization to go and when they need to be there and can engage his team members by painting a picture of what it will look like (for both the organization and individuals) when they get there. An outstanding leader knows who his team members are and what each of them brings to the table and he engages them according to their abilities and expertise. Finally, an outstanding leader leads the celebration when the team accomplishes wins or milestones—both minor and major."

TOM MCNOWN, MANAGER, TRAINING & MARKETING
GENERAL MOTORS OF CANADA LIMITED

Pierre Nadeau, Vice President of the National Dairy Council in Canada felt that there really is no single universal definition of a leader. Instead he thought that the success of a leader depends on the circumstances surrounding their role—the more complex it is, the more demanding it becomes. He went on to say that "successful leaders cannot be defined only positively. They must have the right combination of positive traits as well as not possess as many or more negative traits. The latter, less appealing category doesn't make for good reading but is very real. Ignoring the negatives can have disastrous effects. No matter how good a leader can be potentially, there are

> **"The visible signs of artful leadership are expressed, ultimately, in its practice."**
>
> MAX DePREE, FORMER CEO
> HERMAN MILLER

faults that can nullify the positive aspects." Faults which can transform leaders into liabilities to themselves, their people, and the cause they seek to serve. An astute observation to always keep in mind.

Given that it is necessary for an effective leader to possess most, if not all, of the qualities described above, a burning question arises. Are leaders "born," or can they be made? Can leadership be learned and taught? Can we become the leaders we would want to work for?

Warren Bennis, a professor at the University of Southern California's business school, declared unequivocally that leadership can't be taught, since "leadership is character and judgment — and two things you can't teach are judgment and character."

Many disagree. One of the more blatantly outspoken opponents was legendary professional football coach Vince Lombardi, who believed leaders were not born. "Leaders are made, and they are made by effort and hard work." Many other leaders concur. In a recent interview, Michael Dell, Chairman and CEO of Dell Computers, commented that "natural non-leaders don't exist. Everyone has some degree of leadership capability, but it depends

> **"At the company car wash, the outstanding leader can't be seen because he is busy scrubbing the undercarriage of the car, while members of his/her team are being praised lavishly for giving it such a beautiful shine."**
>
> ROSS P. LEDERER, DIRECTOR OF BUSINESS DEVELOPMENT
> CRAFT-BILT MANUFACTURING COMPANY

on whether they want to develop it." Thomas P. Gerrity, of the University of Pennsylvania agrees "Anyone can advance their leadership skills…no matter where their abilities fall on the spectrum from 'natural leader' to 'natural non-leader.' "

I wholeheartedly throw my support behind the latter opinions. While there are certainly born leaders, leadership can indeed be learned and taught to others. One becomes a leader when one does the work of a leader. It can be done! It just takes the drive, the know-how and the vision to do it.

THE INTERCONNECTIVITY OF LEADERSHIP

The essence of leadership can be viewed graphically as four interconnected diamonds, each interdependent on the others, each joined by the influence of the leader, the needs of the individuals and their ties to the enterprise.

"The key to successful leadership today is influence, not authority."

KENNETH H. BLANCHARD, CHAIRMAN
BLANCHARD TRAINING AND DEVELOPMENT INC.

Of the ten characteristics itemized on pages one and two, check off the ones you consider your strengths. Place an asterisk beside those you consider your weaknesses.

Would you work for you?   Yes ☐ No ☐ I'm not sure at this time ☐

SOME TOUGH QUESTIONS

1. **What is your definition of a leader?**

    _____

    _____

2. **Of the people you know, who embodies that definition?
    How close are you to being the leader of your own definition?**

    _____

    _____

3. **Why do you think the ability to inspire is considered the
    most important leadership quality among many leaders? What do you
    do that inspires and motivates others?**

    _____

    _____

4.   What would you rank as the most important quality of a leader? Why?

_____

_____

_____

5.   How effective are your communication skills? How do you know?
     What feedback have you asked for and received?

_____

_____

_____

_____

6.   What do you feel are your leadership strengths? How have you verified
     that your perception is accurate? What can you do to further enhance
     your strengths?

_____

_____

_____

_____

7.   What are your leadership weaknesses? What evidence do you have of them?
     What can you do to begin to eliminate these weaknesses?

_____

_____

_____

_____

8. Do you accept there are some things you're just not good at, and put
    people who are good at them in your place? What are the results?

    _____

    _____

    _____

    _____

9. What leadership requirement that didn't make the Top Ten would you
    include? Why?

    _____

    _____

    _____

    _____

10. Explain why you checked off "yes," "no" or "I'm not sure at this time" above.

    _____

    _____

    _____

    _____

CHAPTER 2

MIRROR MIRROR ON THE WALL

Would You Work for You?
*Yes, if Only... **You Know Yourself***

Of course you know yourself! You would recognize yourself anywhere. However being really aware of who you are—knowing what is of utmost importance to you, realizing where your strengths and weaknesses lie, being conscious of how your value system stacks up and managing your inner self— is more complicated and has more far reaching implications than might appear at first glance.

BECOMING MORE AWARE

The primary objective of this chapter is to assist you to recognize and manage your own emotions effectively. To many readers this may sound too touchy-feely to be business oriented. Let me assure you that this is not the case—just the opposite is true. Being more aware of yourself, managing yourself better, is of inestimable importance especially when you are the leader. Extensive research bears this out, as we shall see. If you didn't know who you really were, would you want to work for you? Would anyone else?

Leaders have been applauded for their brainpower and their technical skills for many years. No one would deny

> "For this is the journey that men make: to find themselves. If they fail in this, it doesn't matter much what else they find."
>
> JAMES A. MICHENER (1907-1997)
> AUTHOR

that intelligence and cognitive skills are essential for outstanding leadership. However, studies by the late David McClelland and more recently by Daniel Goleman indicate emphatically that emotional intelligence (EI), that is, recognizing and managing our own feelings and behaviors, have profound influence on our effectiveness as leaders. More to the point, Dr. Goleman found that emotional intelligence proved to be twice as important as technical skills and IQ for jobs at all levels. For top leaders it accounts for 85 to 90% of a star performance.

For 515 senior executives analyzed by the search firm Egon Zehnder International, it was found that emotional intelligence (EI) was a better predictor of success than either relevant previous experience or high IQ. It was found that executives with high EI were involved in 74% of organizational successes and only 24% of failures. The study found results to be almost identical in the three cultures (Latin America, Germany, Japan) studied.

"We know what we are, not what we may become."
WILLIAM SHAKESPEARE (1564-1616)
PLAYWRIGHT, POET

THE IMPORTANCE OF SELF AWARENESS

Carl Rodgers and other humanistic psychologists in the 1950s, 60s and 70s discussed the importance of self-awareness. They opined that "being aware" or being "fully functioning" were among the keys to building a realistic view of ourselves, and from there building a realistic view of those with whom we make contact. Individuals who are self-aware seldom experience great inconsistency between the way they see themselves and the way other people see them. They are likely to deal with new or adjustive experiences realistically without much anxiety or discomfort and without the need to "go on the defensive." Although Rodgers felt it was unlikely anyone would achieve the pinnacle of self-awareness, it was nonetheless the ideal toward which to strive. He added that this search is "not for the faint hearted. It involves the stretching and growing of becoming more and more of one's potentialities… it means launching oneself fully into the stream of life." Rodgers contended that self-aware persons exhibit ten characteristics that would make you want to work for them.

RODGERS' TEN CHARACTERISTICS OF A SELF-AWARE, FULLY FUNCTIONING PERSON

1. An open-mindedness to new experiences without being defensive.

2. The ability to change without fear in response to new experiences.

3. The ability to demonstrate trust in themselves and their feelings, to do what "feels right," trust their gut instinct.

4. The ability to seek out new experiences, new challenges willingly.

5. Regard themselves positively and accept themselves.

6. Have a positive regard for others and accept them.

7. Maintain a sense of being in control of their own lives, responsible for own actions.

8. Their lives may be described as enriched, exciting, rewarding, challenging, meaningful.

9. They are always stretching and developing more of their capabilities.

10. They live life fully, striving forward.

Measure yourself against the characteristics in Rodgers' list. In which areas do you feel you would benefit from improvement?

Consider the tremendous value of taking a realistic view of yourself. From a leadership perspective it helps if you see yourself as you really are because this is how others are most likely to see you. Becoming fully self-aware involves recognizing our skills, abilities, values, needs and goals. It involves appreciating our own individual qualities: our intelligence…confidence… shyness… imagination. Of course, to be at all valuable, our self-awareness must also involve confronting those negative aspects of our characters which could adversely affect our capabilities as leaders. These include impatience, intolerance, intransigence and lack of empathy. We then become aware of our interpersonal styles, our motives, assumptions and coping mechanisms. The benefits to our business of such an outlook are immeasurable.

> "What future leaders have to recognize is they have to know themselves extremely well in order to continue to build their capability and bring value to their industries."
> CATHY WALT & ALISDAIR ROBERTSON, RESEARCHERS
> ANDERSEN CONSULTING

Just imagine how these principles might work in practice. As a highly self-aware leader, you decide to alter your schedule so that instead of arriving at work around 9:30 am, you get into the office at 7:00 am. Very soon you find that you're accomplishing more in those two-and-a-half hours than you used to in an entire day.

As a highly self-aware leader, you ask for assistance in "crunching the numbers" because your strength is marketing, not accounting.

> "One of the most difficult challenges a leader faces today is not having all the answers to the questions being asked."
> HENRY VEENEMA, SENIOR MANAGER,
> CORPORATE GENERAL AFFAIRS
> CANON CANADA INC.

As a highly self-aware leader, you let your very demanding client do most of the talking and complaining, while you do most of the listening and acquiescing, because you realize they need the chance to "get it out of their system."

As a highly self-aware leader, you realize your own worth to an organization and expect a competitive salary. However you are ready to let a very highly paid job go by because you know you will be unhappy working in a huge impersonal firm.

As a highly self-aware leader, you are comfortable talking about your strengths and weaknesses, and often look for constructive criticism in order to improve. Those who are not self-aware see the need to improve as a threat or a sign of failure.

Can your degree of self-awareness be altered? Certainly! Are you born with a certain level of self-awareness that will remain with you for life? Of course not!

Child psychologists have, for years, affirmed that people are born with their own degree of personal self-awareness. It can however be increased with determination and concentrated effort. The necessary first step is wanting to change. The second step is to practice the new level of awareness by asking yourself reflective questions. The third step is to solicit feedback from those around you to determine if you have been successful. Finally you must continue to practice, until you naturally recognize your enhanced awareness and respond in tandem with it. It is a long-term effort, but the rewards to both your business life and your personal life are so substantial it is certainly worth doing.

"The job of leadership today is not just to make money. It's to make meaning."
JOHN SEELY BROWN, DIRECTOR
XEROX PARC

"If my first attempt to solve a problem doesn't work, I simply try to understand where I have gone wrong and then make adjustments. The key to doing something right may lie in the feedback you get from doing something wrong."
DR. AN WANG, FOUNDER
WANG LABORATORIES, INC.

TEN STEPS TO DEVELOP ACCURATE SELF-PERCEPTION

1. *Know Your Strengths and Weaknesses.*

   Get to really know yourself, from the inside, out. Take action to enhance your listening skills, your motivation, your empathy for others—or whatever needs improving.

2. *Focus Particularly on the Business Aspects You Want to Improve.*

   Imagine a real business situation in which your heightened emotional skills would be beneficial. For example, by using a more intuitive listening approach to everyone in meetings, colleagues and subordinates alike, the number of options brought up for discussion could be greatly enhanced.

3. *Assess Your Behavior in Important Situations.*

   Do you react differently to different people—your family, business associates, workers? Do you react differently in different situations? Do all your reactions bring out the best in each situation? Are you patient? Relaxed? Distracted? Bored? Why? What can you do to make your behavior more consistent —more positive?

4. *Emulate a Role Model.*

   Look for someone who is self-aware, who listens well, whose passions encourage others and whose drive is an excellent example to follow. Watch closely how they interact with others. Visualize yourself in their role—and picture the way you would conduct yourself in similar circumstances. "Patterning" is an excellent method to change existing behavior into new, more desirable behavior.

5. *Ask for Feedback.*

Solicit input from colleagues, staff, friends and family. Accept their comments
as observations and suggestions toward improvement—not as criticism. Keep
in mind that others see you from a different perspective and, in many cases a
much more objective perspective than you see yourself. Research has
corroborated this—finding a much higher correlation between the accuracy of
feedback and the reality of the situation than there is between your own
impression of it and the reality. Considering the feedback of others widens the
window through which you see yourself.

6. *Keep a Journal.*

Document observations and efforts to change. Regard lapses as learning
experiences. Regard small improvements as triumphs. Reread old journal
entries to remind yourself of the progress you've made. This method broadens
and clarifies perception very quickly.

7. *Practice. Practice. Practice.*

New behavior patterns take time to become automatic. One day you'll find you
no longer need to think about the behavior you've tried to establish; it's just
there. But be patient. It takes persistence.

8. *Ask the Right Questions.*

Answers to the "right" questions require reflection and a willingness to
improve. Ask "why?" questions. Why am I leading the way I am? Why do I make
the decisions I do? Why do I get angry—impatient? If I were to leave the
organization, what would be the reaction among my colleagues, and staff?

9. *Work Toward Your Goal.*

Take the "eulogy" test. What do you want said about you when you "shuffle off this mortal coil?" Write it down. Start making the changes necessary to be the person you want to be remembered as. Shortly after I had completed this section of the chapter, I came across this tribute in the *Globe & Mail:*

> *In memoriam*
> *Robert J. Humphrey*
> *1947 – 2000*
> *Chairman and CEO, Harry Rosen*
>
> *In 1975 Bob Humphrey gave Harry Rosen a gift, he joined the company. He was the perfect fit. On Sunday July 23rd, he passed away. We need no special words to express our true feelings for our Chairman; honest ones will do just fine. For twenty five years he was the heart of this company. His brilliance, his leadership, his ability to get things done compelled us forward. His humanity and friendship made it fun. A list of his personal and professional achievements would produce a staggering quantity, all the more impressive for its quality. He was driven to succeed, but as everyone here whose lives he touched would readily attest, he kept no clock when it came to sharing himself with others. When you hold up a mirror to his life, it does more than reflect a brilliant career, it brings into focus a truly unique man. We miss you. Your family, at Harry Rosen.*

There is no greater praise for a leader.

10. *Take a Flexible Approach.*

Recognize that the person you are now is not the same person you were last year or will be next year. The environment, our circumstances, our relationships are evolving—they demand change, flexibility. Remember yourself as you were yesterday, know yourself as you are today and anticipate yourself as you will be tomorrow. Do the same for all those with whom you come in contact.

"The real voyage of discovery is not seeking new lands, but in seeing with new eyes."

MARCEL PROUST, (1871-1922)
AUTHOR

When asked, leaders agreed: it took months of effort to succeed in their endeavor to perceive themselves more accurately and manage themselves more effectively. Along the way, the leaders with whom I spoke had the courage to ask themselves:

- ◆ **What is my purpose in being a leader?**

- ◆ **Where do my passions lie?**

- ◆ **What weaknesses do I see in myself?**

- ◆ **How vulnerable am I to these flaws?**

- ◆ **What am I doing to eliminate them?**

- ◆ **What are my goals?**

THE INTERDEPENDENCE OF PERCEPTION

Perception, the ability to "see" not only ourselves, but everyone around us, is essential because our behavior stems from it. We perceive what we want to see, what we've always seen, what we expect to see and what makes sense to us. Perception, in short, is based on what fits into our understanding of the way the world should be, until something happens to change one of these parameters. This is obviously a very personal process. However, by taking a step back to really look at ourselves, our staff and our environment, in a dispassionate, honest light we have the unique and rewarding opportunity to greatly enlarge our viewing platform and hence find an increased variety of methods for responding to situations in the workplace.

THE INTERDEPENDENCE OF PERCEPTION

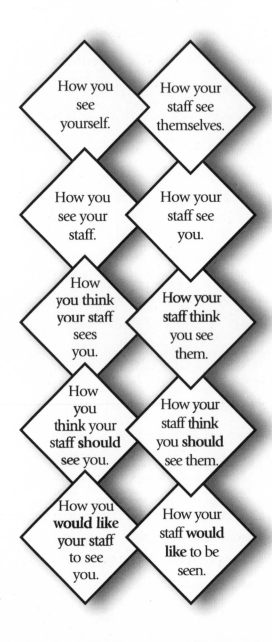

Consider how interdependent perception is.

> How you see yourself... is connected to
>
> How you see others... which is connected to
>
> How you think others see you... which is connected to
>
> How you think others should see you... which is connected to
>
> How you would like to be seen.

In the work environment the interconnectivity of perception is even greater because...

> How your staff see themselves... is connected to
>
> How your staff see you... which is connected to
>
> How your staff think you see them... which is connected to
>
> How your staff think you should see them... which is connected to
>
> How your staff would like to be seen... which is connected to
>
> How you see yourself...

Complicated? No wonder perception is so inaccurate.

Some leaders are to be envied for their outstanding perception. They know themselves, their staff, their organizations well—unlike many technical skills, accurate perception doesn't take years to learn—just a lifetime to maintain.

RECOGNIZE A SELF-MOTIVATED LEADER

Doug Ivester, former Chairman of Coca-Cola, asked himself leadership-oriented questions. It was said of him that everything he touched has improved dramatically. Whatever target he sets, he hits. More than ten years ago Ivester set himself—in writing—the date for his goal to become CEO and Chairman of Coca-Cola. He was not far off. It took him only two years longer to achieve his objective.

He, like other successful leaders, has the internal motivation to achieve for the glory of achievement—rather than being motivated only by a big salary or high status.

Motivation leads you forward. It assists you to set realistic yet challenging goals, it monitors your risk taking. It facilitates performance excellence. Highly motivated people are always raising their own performance bars. They stretch, recognizing their limits yet refusing to settle for easily attainable victories. They are committed to the task, to the company, to their teammates.

Ask yourself what motivates you? What turns you on? What keeps your light lit? What encourages you to continue in the face of obstacles?

We all know the BIG self-motivated leaders—like Bill Gates, Anthony Robbins, Oprah Winfrey and Mary Kay Ash. We can also recognize and appreciate those self-motivated leaders closer to home.

One of my all-time favorites is Terry Fox, a cancer fighter, who, while attempting to run across Canada from coast-to-coast, inspired and mobilized an entire nation. Such iron willed motivation is attainable for all of us, but most of us need a little push. I asked several highly motivated leaders for suggestions on how to jump start one's own internal drive. These are some of their responses.

BECOME A SELF-MOTIVATED LEADER

Use the "Little Engine That Could" Mantra.

From early childhood we remember the saga of the little engine that used all its positive determination to carry its passengers up the highest mountain. All along the way it puffed "I think I can. I think I can. I think I can." Our minds are powerful. They reinforce either negative thoughts (I can't) or positive thoughts (I can). Motivate yourself by documenting "I can" precepts in your daytimer, in your journal or in your palm pilot. These might be notes such as, "I can make five follow-up calls today" or "I can get an appointment to demonstrate my new idea today" or "I can organize and write the operational manual by the deadline." Look at them everyday—work toward them everyday—and they'll become your positive mantra to success.

> **"Whether you think you can or can't—you are right."**
> HENRY FORD, (1863-1947),
> FOUNDER & PRESIDENT
> FORD MOTOR COMPANY

Practice Makes Perfect.

Life truly is a self-fulfilling prophecy—you become what you believe you'll become. By capitalizing on your strengths—by motivating yourself to succeed, you will. Do you practice what you want to happen or what you would like to avoid? Do you often repeat "I wish I had more time, more money, more friends, more motivation?" Stop wishing and start making more time, more money, more friends, more motivation.

Focus on Small. Focus on One.

Eliminating all of a company's problems by next Friday, is a bit of a challenge. Improving slowly, quarter by quarter, is an achievable goal. Take the time to prioritize the order with which problems should be dealt. Focus on each of the steps—one at a time. It's a much more manageable and rewarding approach. After his gold medal triathalon performance in the Sidney 2000 Olympics, an interviewer asked Canadian Simon Whitfield where he found "the stuff" to test himself harder than he ever had before. Whitfield replied, "I asked myself how much I wanted the gold medal—and then focused all my energy on this one task—getting it."

> **"Your goals should be just out of reach but not out of sight."**
> ANONYMOUS

Prioritize. Re-prioritize.

It's easy to become overwhelmed by the unending stream of "emergencies" that seem to develop overnight. Take a minute each morning to re-focus on what is really important—what is most important. Keep priorities and motivation intact. You have the freedom to choose what you consider *most important*. Once you've done that, make sure your focus, your actions and your goals are aligned.

Conduct "Search and Adapt Exercises."

Look for examples of self-motivated leaders. Read about their strategies and techniques for staying on track, and for maintaining their drive. Find ways to copy, emulate, and adapt their techniques and strategies. Document your discoveries. Record your adaptive techniques. Critique your progress.

Warren Buffet, advocated "search and adapt" as a solution for smart people who interfere with their own success. He advised them to write down admirable qualities and then practice them until they become habit-forming. His next comment is well worth remembering, *"The chains of habit are too light to be felt until they are too heavy to be broken."*

RELATING TO OTHERS

The 60s refrain of "no man is an island—no man stands alone" from a John Donne poem, rings in my head as I write this. For leaders in the 21st Century this song is tremendously relevant, since no one can survive in isolation. They must be members of the team, utilizing everyone's abilities, to work toward a common goal and to achieve the maximum potential.

How well do you relate to those around you? As a leader do you have the wisdom to know when to lead, when to follow and when to get out of the way? Research at the Center for Creative Leadership has found that the primary causes of derailment in executives involve difficulty in handling change, not being able to work well in a team and poor inter-personal relations.

> "Since management is getting work done through others, an outstanding leader is one who can envision the future, motivate and delegate to qualified people —then stay the hell out of the way! A leader is one who instills pride and confidence in an organization."
>
> BERNIE BRILL, EXECUTIVE VICE PRESIDENT SMART

A while back I heard a story related by an anthropologist. Its powerful message has remained with me for years.

Travelling by jeep through the jungles of South America, her small party was held up by a gang of rebels. At gunpoint they were told to line up away from the jeep while everything was taken out of it. One man in the group began talking to the rebel leader, casually—schmoozing. As he spoke and joked, he slowly began to put everything back into the jeep. When the moment of decision arrived for the rebel leader, he just shrugged, took a few things and sent the group on its way.

Recalling the incident, the anthropologist felt that although she spoke the language of the country, the man in the group who had taken action spoke the culture. He recognized the underlying patterns of interaction between people. Understanding and utilizing those patterns of interaction accurately and effectively is what defines perceptive leaders.

While few leaders face situations on a daily basis where clear comprehension of "the other point of view" holds life or death consequences, today's leaders are certainly required to intelligently consider the feelings and the history of those with whom they have regular contact in order to make judicious decisions. Although the underlying patterns that exist in relationships are often invisible, cloaked in layers of past and present expectations, an innovative leader is able to "see" into this invisible core and thereby initiate or encourage beneficial interaction.

Being aware of the thoughts, outlook, attitude and expectations of others empowers leaders to anticipate and meet their needs. This level of sensitivity is often not considered businesslike, however research has shown it offers tremendous business benefits.

By thinking with staff, not for them; *by empathizing with them,* not becoming emotionally involved; *by moving with colleagues,* not rushing ahead or dawdling behind; *by working with staff,* not doing things for them; *by accepting them as they are,* not judging and criticizing them; and *by seeing from the other point of view,* not merely from your own, you grow as a leader, your staff grows, your company grows.

Integrate these ten principles into your understanding of human behavior to help make you the empathetic, sensitive leader that people appreciate—and are happy to work for.

UNDERSTANDING HUMAN BEHAVIOUR PRINCIPLES

◆ Everyone "sees" from their own unique perspective, *and it is bound to be different from yours.*

◆ Everyone wants to be fulfilled—to be satisfied—to be happy. They change to gain pleasure. They change to avoid pain.

◆ Living or working in different environments causes people to think and act differently, because their experiences, and hence their perception of reality, is different.

◆ No matter how illogical, strange or irrational some behavior appears to the observer, it makes sense to the person exhibiting it—and it is, at that moment, fulfilling to them.

◆ True understanding comes primarily from experience. A decided course of action is appreciated by those who assisted in its formulation.

> "A leader must be able to 'fire' people up."
>
> LORNE CAMPBELL, VICE PRESIDENT, GROCERY OPERATIONS THRIFTY FOODS

◆ Feelings and emotions are often far more powerful than rational judgment.

◆ True cooperation is possible only in a win-win situation. The benefits and the rewards must be appreciated and be attainable by all.

◆ The methods used to garner cooperation may be more significant than the cooperation itself.

◆ Feelings and attitudes change when people convince themselves that change is beneficial to them—not before.

◆ The best perspective from which to understand the perceptions, attitudes and behavior of those you lead, is from each person's internal frame of reference.

EMPATHY HUMANIZES. COMPASSION UPLIFTS.

Reinforcing what I have always believed, recent studies at PepsiCo showed that division leaders around the world with emotional strengths such as self-awareness, adaptability, and empathy outperformed their targets by 15–20%. Those lacking in these areas, underperformed their targets by approximately the same percentage.

In today's hi-tech, global business environment empathy has become a more vital component of effective leadership than ever before. When dealing with people from around the world, it is essential to be cognizant of the nuances of different cultures and make every effort to demonstrate empathetic savvy. During a program I delivered to the American Society of Travel Agents (ASTA) in Strasbourg, France, I met a couple who reaffirmed the importance of empathy in everyday business life. They trained European business people in the cultural niceties of business in America at their offices in Paris—and educated American business people in European know-how at their offices in Cincinnati. They explained that with so much at stake in the global business scene, leaders wanted to prevent the *faux pas* that plagued many earlier international business efforts.

Being empathetic in one-to-one relationships is a difficult task; in a group environment where each member has individual quirks it becomes even more problematic. With the ever increasing use of teams in business, it is a skill certainly worth mastering now. I remember speaking to a health organization that was trying to change their business model. Staff were having problems acclimatizing to the changes. Instead of being responsible for only their own patients, they were jointly responsible for all patients. They had a difficult time establishing for themselves where their responsibilities began and ended. They felt they had to keep track of so many patients it was overwhelming. The CEO understood their concerns and together with the staff supervisor developed several systems to assist in handling the new situation. After discussion with the staff one of the systems was modified and introduced. As the supervisor had realized, staff appreciated that their input was requested and utilized. While the system required finessing and adjusting, it was accepted and later became a model for other home care organizations.

I recently read a customer service article that described how the general manager of a prestigious hotel, while overseeing a black tie function noticed one uncomfortable dignitary without the *de rigeur* tuxedo. The hotel manager took the man to his *maitre d'*, who not only handed him the tuxedo off his own back but had it quickly altered to fit. The guest was able to enjoy himself at the function in appropriate style—and the general manager collected kudos for his excellent service. In my opinion, the general manager had gone beyond excellent service to excellent empathy—a leadership quality greatly appreciated by all who bump into it.

Empathetic and compassionate leadership facilitates not only better employee performance, it contributes significantly to optimized job satisfaction and decreased turnover rate.

TRUST BINDS

One of the major forces in any relationship is trust. Remember the flying trapeze artists at the circus; trust is encoded into the relationship that allows them to work together. It is no different in a business organization. Nearly 65% of American Human Resources managers surveyed by the Conference Board, N.Y., cited mistrust of management as the biggest obstacle in employer/employee relations. Distrustful workers are less committed and less effective than those who trust their employers. Distrustful managers waste time checking up on employees and are also less effective as a result.

Leaders who are of exemplary character are "mirror-testworthy." They can look at themselves and be satisfied with the image they see. They can feel the trust and confidence that others reflect back at them and set an example for the rest of the organization.

> "I refuse to see a pimp in the mirror in the morning when I shave."
>
> GERMAN AMBASSADOR IN LONDON, 1906

A CREDO TO MAINTAIN TRUST

- ◆ Be absolutely truthful. Demonstrate it.
- ◆ Trust your associates. Show it.
- ◆ Be willing to accept new ideas, no matter their source.
- ◆ Take personal risks for the sake of the company.
- ◆ Give credit where it's due.
- ◆ Be absolutely honest with money.
- ◆ Put the interest of others before your own.
- ◆ Coach freely.

—Researchers at the University of Chicago's Social Psychological Department

The surveys on the next page beg some questions of those who are examining themselves and their business relationships. Are you honest? Open minded? Keep promises? Are you respectful? Do you share information? Does your trusting attitude show? How can you demonstrate you are of such exemplary character that you would work for you?

> "Walk the Talk."
>
> ALMOST EVERY LEADER WITH WHOM I SPOKE.

TRUST MAKERS

◆ Maintain integrity (58% of those surveyed agreed)

◆ Openly communicate vision and values (51%)

◆ Show respect for fellow employees as equal partners (47%)

◆ Focus on shared goals more than on personal agendas (38%)

◆ Do the right thing regardless of personal risk (36%)

◆ Listen with an open mind (33%)

◆ Demonstrate caring compassion (22%)

◆ Maintain confidences (15%)

TRUST BREAKERS

◆ Act inconsistently in what they say and do (69%)

◆ Seek personal gain above shared gain (41%)

◆ Withhold information (34%)

◆ Lie or tell half-truths (33%)

◆ Are close-minded (29%)

◆ Are disrespectful to employees (28%)

◆ Withhold support (16%)

◆ Break promises (14%)

◆ Betray confidences (13%)

— Manchester Inc.
Survey of executives at 215 companies

LEAD FROM A POSITION OF SELF CONTROL

"Self-reference, self-knowledge, self-control; these three alone lead life to sovereign power."

LORD ALFRED TENNYSON
OENONE, 1832

"Leadership is defined by what you do, not who you are."

WILBERT L. "BILL" GORE, FOUNDER
W.L. GORE & ASSOCIATES

"Make it thy business to know thy self, which is the most difficult lesson in the world."

MIGUEL DE CERVANTES, (1547-1616)
AUTHOR

Leaders who are in control create a calmer, more reasonable environment. Self-control has a trickle-down effect. It prevents panic. It promotes fairness. In rapidly changing times, a cool collected approach is preferable to hasty decisions made when emotions run high and rational thinking runs low. Leaders who demonstrate their self-control with reflection, thoughtfulness and level-headedness send clear messages to all those around them that their actions are not impulsive, but carefully calculated. This is a reassuring and confidence building perception for staff and colleagues.

Contemplate your own ability to stay in control. How well are you able to handle stress? How reassuring are you to others?

A retail study by Lusch & Serpkeuci found that the most successful store managers are those best able to handle stress. (Success was based on net profits, sales per square foot, sales per employee and inventory investment).

Rereading this chapter has made me acutely aware that knowing yourself—really knowing who you are—has everything to do with business leadership and nothing to do with business leadership. Becoming a more self-aware and perceptive person has everything to do with life no matter where and with whom you live it. The precepts outlined in the chapter are for everyone, everywhere. To know thyself precedes the ability to know anyone else.

Would you work for you?   Yes ☐   No ☐   I'm not sure at this time ☐

SOME TOUGH QUESTIONS

1. What assumptions do I bring with me when I interact with others
    (supervisors, co-workers, family, staff, etc)? What attitudes do I bring
    with me? Are they helpful? Constructive?

    _____

    _____

    _____

    _____

2. What do I expect of others (supervisors, co-workers, family, staff, etc)?
    Are my expectations realistic?

    _____

    _____

    _____

3. What is my greatest strength? Biggest weakness?

    _____

    _____

    _____

    _____

4. What in my behavior wins respect? Alienates others?

_____

_____

_____

5. Do I demonstrate a constructive and stimulating manner in dealing with others?

_____

_____

_____

_____

_____

6. What is my reputation with others (supervisors, co-workers, family, staff, etc)?

_____

_____

_____

_____

7. What do people like about me and my behavior? What do they dislike?

_____

_____

_____

_____

8. What do I like about myself? Dislike about myself?

_____

_____

_____

9. What causes me problems in dealing with others (supervisors,
    co-workers, family, staff, etc)?

    _____

    _____

    _____

    _____

    _____

10. What interpersonal strategies do I use most often in my relationships
    with others (supervisors, co-workers, family, staff, etc)?

    _____

    _____

    _____

    _____

    _____

Chapter 3

Up Close and Personal

Would You Work for You?
*Yes, if Only... **You Know Your People***

Once you have become more aware of yourself, your needs and wants, you are better able to focus on your people. To get good people, to keep them, to ensure they will want to work for you, it is essential to know who they really are, what they really want and need, what their attitudes are.

EVERYONE WANTS JOB QUALITY AND WORKPLACE SUPPORT

The 1997 National Study of the Changing Workforce (NSCW), indicated that everybody generally looks for the same job satisfiers: higher job quality and workplace support.

Job quality, as defined by the NSCW, incorporates autonomy on the job, learning opportunties, meaningfulness of work, opportunity for advancement and job security. *Workplace support* is defined as flexibility in work arrangements, supervisor assistance, supportive company culture, positive co-worker relations, absence of discrimination,

"Today when people work for a company, they want to know, what's in it for me?"

CAROLYN CLARK, VICE PRESIDENT, HUMAN RESOURCES
FAIRMONT HOTELS & RESORTS

"The No. 1 factor in job satisfaction is doing meaningful work."

SANDY FRENCH, PRESIDENT
NORTHERN LIGHTS COMMUNICATIONS GROUP

respect in the workplace and equal opportunity for workers of all backgrounds.

The NSCW findings are extremely pertinent for today's leaders. Whereas traditional belief holds that salary and benefits are at the top of an employee's "most wanted" list, the NSCW found that to maximize employee satisfaction, thereby increasing their commitment to employer and decreasing turnover, employers need to provide high-quality jobs, no matter the occupation, as well as supportive workplace environments, no matter the industry.

Study after study indicate there is dollar and cents value in satisfying employees—in encouraging them to stay. Frederick Reichheld, author of *The Loyalty Effect*, offers up hard statistics that corroborate that a seasoned employee is two or three times as productive as someone just walking in the door. A Watson Wyatt Worldwide study states that replacing an employee costs about 1.5 times a year's salary. This study also finds that companies with highly committed employees tend to post sharply higher shareholder returns, demonstrating enhanced shareholder confidence. The satisfaction level of employees has tremendous impact on their bottom line productivity.

> "Important as it (pay) is, it's probably not the most important factor. I think what employees are looking for in organizations today is a sense of purpose of the organization. We all think we can make a contribution. Each person is motivated to create additional value."
>
> PREM BENIMADHU, DIRECTOR,
> COMPENSATION RESEARCH CENTRE
> CONFERENCE BOARD OF CANADA

NSCW findings indicate that employees in less supportive workplaces with more difficult or more demanding jobs, exhibit much greater levels of negative spillover from work into their home life, thereby jeopardizing their personal and family well-being. This situation has a

> "Every time you hire a leader who doesn't maximize people's potential, you lose market share."
>
> TOM BLACK, PRESIDENT
> PRIVATE BUSINESS INC.

domino effect, because burned-out workers who bring their displeasure home not only sour their personal time, but carry these feelings back again to the workplace, limiting their on-job performance.

"Customer satisfaction starts with employee satisfaction."

Charlie P. Crockett, Sales Director, Automotive Aftermarket Division 3M

FINDING SATISFACTION ACROSS DEMOGRAPHIC LINES

While people across all demographic boundaries search for job quality and workplace support, they don't all "see" these job satisfiers from the same perspective. It is interesting to note that needs, wants and attitudes in many cases are demographically specific.

The oldest workers in the workforce today belong to the demographic group referred to as the Silent Generation, born between 1925 and 1942. They are children of the Depression, greatly affected by their history and the hardships of their time. Sons and daughters who were taught by their mothers and fathers to obey. As they entered the workforce they demonstrated their learned obedience. Their learned loyalty accompanied their belief that their "superiors" knew better than they did. Corporate loyalty was returned to them—to many in the form of a gold watch for their years and years of service.

The Silent Generation understood and accepted this well-established hierarchy of business. It was comforting. Everyone knew exactly where they stood and how they fit into the business structure. It was accepted that if you did your job well, you would climb the corporate ladder rung by rung, as those who started before you had done. You accepted the clearly and formally demarcated lines between bosses and employees—formal lines that supported this hierarchical system. Needs and wants and attitudes were quite simple: to be treated as your station befit; to be compensated fairly for your efforts; to be given the opportunity in the distant future (when you were older) to move into the distinct rank of the "seniors." Their motto was "an honest day's work for an honest day's pay"—and they believed it.

The Baby Boomers, (born between 1943 and 1964) were being raised as the pendulum swung fiercely in the opposite direction. They are the bridge between the Silent Generation and the Gen-Xers. During their early work years the hierarchical business model began to crumble as employees became more assertive. Loyalty gradually diminished, first on the part of Corporate America and then on the part of the employee. As Boomers became managers they practiced the values of an egalitarian organization—the sharing of responsibility, a great deal of communication, respect for the autonomy of fellow workers and a participative team-oriented approach. The term boss was not regarded with favor. A CEO friend of mine explained it well when he remarked, "I grew up with an autocratic boss—ruling from the top down. There were always winners and losers and the outcome was not necessarily for the good of the company. That's not how I see my role—my responsibilities. I'm not interested in being a boss, a lord over my people. What gives me satisfaction is the achievements of the organization as a whole—decisions made by the individuals who make up the organization. When both my staff and I are involved in the decision making process, we arrive at a better solution."

Who works in your organization? What do they need? What do they want?

Gen-Xers, (born between 1965 and 1981), have even more outspoken attitudes and well-articulated demands than their Boomer parents. They have moved even further away from leadership as it was practiced 50 years ago. Looking for a balance between their work life and their home life, they are not willing to sacrifice everything for the job, since they feel that were they to do so there wouldn't be anything left over for their families at the end of the day. Conscious of the huge divorce rate of the boomers they want a more traditional home life than their parents had—they want more time with their partners and children. To them life is first—work is second. Their desire for balance is not without conflict, since they long for "interesting" work, which is often accompanied by long hours; nevertheless they still want their weekends for family time. What can you do to offer your valuable people more of the flexibility they require to satisfactorily integrate the demands of career and the joys of home?

> "One of the most difficult challenges a leader faces today is getting and maintaining a competent staff."
> Kim Struble, CMP, Director, Meetings & Expositions American Logistics Association

Organizations such as Microsoft, Microstrategy, WRQ and QUALCOMM which employ a large number of Gen-Xers, claim they know what their staff wants and are providing it. Work environments that create the impression of an extended university atmosphere, coupled with staff amenities, encourage the acceptance of working long hours. Perks include fitness centers, tuition reimbursement programs, family cruises, nap rooms and on-site massages. These companies, and many others like them are cognizant of the needs of their employees, and have come to recognize that the preferred environment of Gen-Xers, in particular, is a community setting. With so little time to find a sense of community outside of the work environment, employers build that sense of community into the workplace environment in an attempt to satisfy their people.

As needs change with demographic membership, it certainly behooves leaders to be well aware where their people fit and respond accordingly. Keep in mind however that demographics is only one of the factors that

> "How can I lead my people if I do not know where they are going?"
> Anonymous

determines who your employees are and not all employees within any demographic group have identical wants, needs and expectations.

FINDING SATISFACTION ACROSS SALARY LINES

Other significant factors to consider include employee level of education, facility with English, and cultural frame of reference. Recent immigrants, workers with little education and those with poor English skills also have expectations from their job. Until recently employees in the low paying service sector—hotels, restaurants, maintenance—have struggled, often unsuccessfully, to make their voices heard. However, with the drop in unemployment in the U.S. to just over 5%, the situation has changed. In order to manage this workforce, it is necessary to take into account their particular wants and needs (it is estimated by the Economy Policy Institute that nearly 30% of all U.S. employees earn less than $7.50 an hour).

> "Companies are not really doing an effective job of polling their employees and looking at what would keep them."
>
> PETER ANDREWS, PRESIDENT
> TALENTMAP.COM

Aware of this situation, Marriott International, for example, includes a wide variety of incentives in its contract to attract and keep workers, such as employee stock options, social services referral network, daycare, training and ESL (English as a Second Language) classes. Other employers of low-wage workers have realized that they too must satisfy their staff or lose them. ConAgra Prepared Foods started on-site childcare, prenatal care and corporate housing communities when they realized they were experiencing close to 100% annual turnover. JCPenney incorporated flexible shift scheduling when it discovered that seasoned staff—those who remained on the job a year or longer—were 20% more productive. These organizations and many others like them offer special benefits designed to assist employees solve personal problems, in the hope that those problems not spill over into the workplace and thereby decrease productivity— the assumption being that these personal problems are unrelated to their work experiences.

The NSCW however, found just the opposite to be true—work life was actually an important source of the problems. Its report states that "demanding jobs and unsupportive workplaces lead to spillover from jobs into workers' personal life that can create or exacerbate problems off the job that, in turn, spill over into work and diminish productivity. Thus, helping employees to solve problems in their personal lives by providing special programs of assistance—without also reducing the extent to which jobs contribute to these problems—may severely limit the impact of work-life programs on job performance."

While there probably isn't anyone in the workforce who wouldn't accept a raise in pay, surveys continue to show that a good working environment and sense of self-fulfillment is most satisfying and most desired by employees.

Sometimes a single expression of real understanding by an employer may be enough to guarantee a lifetime of loyalty.

Thong Lee, a Marriott bartender, at one time worked in the hotel laundry. He has never forgotten that his boss shut down the laundry on the day of Lee's mother's funeral, so that all of Lee's co-workers could attend.

> "...a good leader must care about their people, being empathetic to their needs, whilst at the same time having passion, drive, energy..."
>
> GRACE CERNIUK, MANAGING DIRECTOR
> RESORTS ONTARIO

Today's hot labor market only intensifies the clout employees hold. After polling two million employees at 700 companies worldwide, Marcus Buckingham of the Gallup Organization found that immediate supervisors are the largest influence on an employee's decision to quit their job. "People leave managers, not companies," he says.

Today the long and the short of it is that if you don't provide employees with what they want, they'll find someone else who will.

> "There are a lot of companies that are just waking up to the fact that there's a war going on out there and it's not just in the hi-tech sector."
>
> KATHY HERTIES, MANAGER, HUMAN RESOURCES
> KPMG LLP

PROVIDING PEOPLE WITH WHAT THEY WANT

1. Provide Opportunity by Training and Enabling

In a recent Gallop poll 15% of American workers said they had the opportunity to use their strengths every day; 69% said they didn't even get to use them once a week.

Opportunity! Career advancement, the chance to work with emerging technology, in

---

EMPLOYEES MOST WANTED LIST

According to a 17-year study of more than 2.4 million workers conducted by International Survey Research (ISR), people want in order:

1. to be treated with uncompromising truth
2. to be trusted by their associates
3. to mentor and be mentored unselfishly
4. management to be receptive to new ideas
5. to be able to take risks without being condemned
6. to receive credit when it is due
7. ethical behavior
8. management to consider the interest of others before its own.

innovative situations. That's why Debra Sandler works for Pepsi. She worked at another company where the boss told her exactly how everything was to be done. Her reaction "I'm an intelligent person and you're paying me a lot of money to make intelligent decisions. Why won't you let me make any decisions? If you want someone who just executes what you want done, you can get someone else to do that. Allow me to contribute." The opportunity to learn new skills and apply them successfully energizes her. What are some of the ways to provide opportunities for your staff?

> **"My ideas and input have always been respected... there's a genuine sincerity, caring and mutual respect among us."**
> JOSIE SCALLITINO, RECEPTIONIST
> ROSENBLUTH INTERNATIONAL

(i) Train

"Training isn't just a nice thing to do anymore," says Laurie Bassi, Vice President of Research at the American Society for Training and Development. "Companies are now thinking of training as a strategic imperative." This is the case for at least two reasons. *First*, employees no longer commit to the same organization for twenty-five years. Most anticipate three or more career changes, precipitated by both personal aspirations and a market fraught with job insecurity. Training is vital to their future marketability. They often make job choices based on the learning and training opportunities available within a particular company. *Secondly*, leaders realize that the ever growing mass of information arriving at incredible speeds on every company's doorstep, can only be absorbed in an environment that advocates on-going learning.

> **"I start with the premise that the function of leadership is to produce more leaders, not followers."**
> RALPH NADER
> CONSUMER ADVOCATE

Given the tremendous importance of training and its invaluable benefits in the form of increased employee knowledge, it should be widespread in North America. But it doesn't seem to be that way… yet. Interestingly, a 1991 *Training* magazine conducted a survey entitled *Rate Your Boss*. Only 56% of respondents rated their bosses as *good to excellent* providers of training opportunities. Have things improved in a decade? Not according to Angela Balan, a Canadian business consultant. She feels that even today, in an age of tremendous competition, few organizations recognize the competitive advantage gained by training employees to maximize these valuable resources. Other business researchers indicate that American businesses are currently spending about 1% of their payroll costs on training, whereas to have a competitive impact in the new millennium a training budget equal to 3% of payroll costs is required.

Some get it. Some don't.

At one end of the spectrum there is the customer who wrote to the Vice President of Merchandising of a major American drugstore chain complaining that when he asked an employee for St. John's Wort, the staffer said it was for treating warts and could be found in the footcare section. "We lost a longtime customer because of the ignorance of an employee," commented the vice president. But whose fault is that? Only by hiring qualified people and providing them with on-going training can we grow.

It behooves every retailer to provide, at a minimum, product training so every employee knows what products are carried and where they are located in the store. An early Saturday morning briefing to inform staff about which products have been added or deleted from inventory and which are specially priced for the weekend certainly makes sense. About a year ago Shoppers Drug Mart, a chain of drugstores in Canada must have instituted a policy indicating that staff are required to take customers right to the product they asked about—not just let them know in which aisle to look. It was great—*while it lasted!*

At the other end of the spectrum is the story of Leonard Roberts, who was hired as Radio Shack Corporation's new president to revitalize the chain. He launched a new advertising campaign with the slogan: "You've got questions, we've got answers"—and to make sure that employees *did indeed* have the answers, he stepped up the training of sales staff, including satellite-delivered Saturday conferences. During these tele-conferences, staff receive the latest in product information, selling and customer service techniques on their in-store monitors. Issues that are forwarded to head office by the stores can easily and quickly be addressed "live" and can also be taped for later viewing and discussion.

> "If you want one year of prosperity, grow grain. If you want ten years of prosperity, grow trees.
> If you want one hundred years of prosperity, grow people."
> CHINESE PROVERB

Advanced Microelectronics Inc., a fast-growing computer services company, learned how essential training is the hard way. It let its employee training program lapse. Productivity soon took a nose-dive as seasoned staff beat a hasty retreat mumbling comments such as "I'm out-of-date" and "I'm not keeping up." Management was taken aback. While there had been internal training programs to teach additional skills in the past, CEO Steve Burkhart didn't realize the enthusiasm employees had for them. His response was to re-establish the program with *even more focus* than before. The result was higher morale and lower turnover. Burkhart now realizes that training is "almost a demanded benefit, or people don't feel like they have a valuable job… it's a big deal for companies—no matter what size they are."

One final tale. Eison Freeman, Inc., a brand promotion agency, (recognizing that its people need the right knowledge, skills and tools to compete) offers a "noontime university" for all its employees. These on-site seminars are taught by experts in advertising and marketing. The company also funds courses for those seeking advanced degrees and those seeking ongoing computer and software training.

> **"We are drowning in information but starved for knowledge."**
> JOHN NAISBITT, CHAIRMAN
> NAISBITT GROUP

Fortune's January 2000 cover story, "The 100 Best Companies to Work For," listed interesting information about each company such as the perks they provide their people. Professional training was seen to be so essential that it stood in a category all its own. Ranked #1, The Container Store provides 135 professional training hours a year. Most of the other companies listed provided upward of forty hours a year.

Talented people get on board in order to learn. They are interested in wages, but they also want intellectual challenge; they want to stand at the frontier of the knowledge economy.

Ask leaders what their biggest challenge is and you get the same answer again and again—finding, attracting and keeping good people. Ask good people what their biggest career challenge is and you get the same answer again and again—finding other good people to work with and work for. In an increasingly tight labor market, providing training—offering learning opportunities—certainly differentiates you from your competitors, makes you want to work for you.

(ii) Enable

> **"An individual without information cannot take responsibility; an individual who is given information cannot help but take responsibility."**
> JAN CARLZON, CEO
> SAS (SWEDEN)

Give employees the ultimate opportunity to do their very best. Training and education empower employees to soar, as does affording them a sense of control over their work. Mike Borg, Marketing Manager for Hewlett-Packard says that "…You don't have to rely on management to make every single decision. We rely on people who are closest to day-to-day activities to make sound decisions, with support and some guidance from management." This philosophy is echoed by managers at other forward thinking organizations.

CONDUCTING EFFECTIVE TRAINING

1.   Make the training convenient. Consider the time constraints of those who require training. Breakfast or lunch training sessions, audio and videotape training sessions are convenient options.

2.   Make the training relevant. Ensure the content relates to the specific job and suits the trainee.

3.   Make training concise. Consider training time as valuable time.

4.   Make training fun. Include interesting examples, innovative exercises.

5.   Make the training on-going. Provide continuous coaching and honest feedback so trainees can incorporate what they've learned into their daily work environment.

6.   Make the training fit individual capabilities. Not everyone learns best in groups; for some one-on-one mentoring, or computer-based training or audio/video tapes are more effective. Provide opportunities for training that fits each trainee.

7.   Make the training program "today" oriented. Focus training on readily applicable skills and knowledge. Keep a path open to continue training along related avenues, over the long term.

8.   Consider the Internet as a training venue. The net opens access to an enormous array of reference materials, seminars, technical reviews and some certification programs. Seminars can be taken via video streamed material which is available any time and in any location. This approach offers many other benefits, including reduced travel and course costs.

When D. Michael Abrashoff, currently Deputy Director for Global Information and Network Systems at U.S. Space and Naval Warfare Systems, was commander of the navy warship, USS Benfold, he looked at enabling and involving staff from a dollar and cents perspective. He felt that the result of having people who were motivated, people who wanted to do the right thing, people who operated more efficiently and more intelligently, improved the bottomline—and that was his goal. Utilizing this grassroots leadership perspective enabled him to boast a significant increase in staff retention and a 75% decrease in operating expenses.

Enabling employees gives you not only their hands, it gives you their brains and hearts as well.

2. Provide A Good Place to Work

A recent Angus Reid Group poll found that nearly half of Canadian employees surveyed experience a great deal of stress at work—25% of them so extreme it makes them ill. It seems workers are having problems coping with their job—their workload—their workplace relationships. The effects of stress are cyclical. It reduces the ability to concentrate, which in turn reduces productivity leading to employer angst, which circles around to create even more stress.

A recent article in the *Globe & Mail* caught my eye. Pregnant women are concerned about how workplace stresses adversely affect their pregnancies. In particular they are worried about whether stress causes premature births, or low birth weight. The chief of obstetrics and gynecology at New York University Downtown Hospital has seen a sharp increase in patients troubled about stress—accounting for up to about one-third of his patients on any given day. In this tight labor market it makes good business sense for leaders to examine their practices surrounding pregnancy as a litmus test for overall workplace quality, particularly where stress is concerned.

Many leaders do recognize the crippling effect of stress on their workforce and have begun to take steps to alleviate it. One company hired a part-time concierge who picks up employees' dry cleaning, runs errands and takes lunch orders. This service makes employees' lives a little easier and leaves them feeling appreciated.

Nova Chemicals Corporation, a Canadian company with plants in Ontario and Alberta, provides a napping room, especially for its shift workers. Power napping reduces the effects of on-the-job stress, increases productivity and decreases safety concerns among those who work long or irregular hours. A 20-minute nap can make all the difference to workers on a twelve-hour shift that ends at 6 am. It can bounce them back to 100% productivity.

Cisco Systems, Inc. recently opened one of the largest daycare centers in the U.S. and ushered in a new age of virtual parenting. The $10 million center enables parents to monitor their children over their office Internet connections and even receive up-to-the-minute e-mail photos while travelling. Cisco employees will now be able to reply with confidence to that oft-asked question, "Do you know where your children are?"

In today's demanding business environment, companies are looking to attract and retain the best talent, better than their competitors do—and some are looking at "fun" in the workplace as a way to accomplish this. "Fun" energizes, and seems to attract and retain valuable employees. Advocates of a fun environment feel that learning, productivity, creativity, morale and *esprit de· corps* are enhanced, while burnout and absenteeism is drastically reduced. They remind the rest of us that friendship and camaraderie are the basic building blocks of the human spirit.

Fast Company magazine reported how Sprint's small business sales

> "People are attracted to the company because working here helps them become better than they could be otherwise."
>
> CHRIS MEYER,
> DIRECTOR OF CENTER FOR BUSINESS INNOVATION
> ERNST & YOUNG

division in Kansas City created a good place to work. To counteract the tedium of eight-hour shifts making cold calls, the team might leave work at 3 pm to go bowling. "After doing something like that," says Nancy Deibler, Manager, "the difference that it makes is measurable and it lasts for weeks. It lifts productivity."

Steve Schwartz, Co-founder and President of Schwartz Communications, a Massachusetts-based organization agrees, "I think having a fun culture is a key element in our recruiting. We know that, because applicants walk around and see happy interactions, and they sense the spirit and energy here. You can almost breathe it in the air, and they want to be a part of that." Like a growing number of firms, Schwartz Communications has no dress code, has pool and ping-pong tables, dart boards and video games. It holds monthly *Thank God it's Thursday* beer-and-pizza parties and occasionally hosts company outings to unusual venues, such as theme parks. According to Schwartz, the environment is an important reason their turnover is low—about one-third the industry average.

Other companies organize a wide variety of activities from fun days and company choir, to cruise trips and "recess." Each company endeavors to harness their employees' natural spirit, then focus that spirit to where it stimulates, bonds and strengthens employees.

3. Provide a Sense of Personal Achievement

More than money is at stake. We choose to work for one company rather than another because the affiliation, the environment, the reason for the work and the work itself, connects intrinsically with our sense of well-being.

We want a place that nurtures our self-esteem. That's why Lisa Shaw works at Whole Foods Market. "I just hang on to the fact that my job is good in some larger sense." Employees at TD Industries are equally upbeat. One says, "this company makes you feel like a human being again."

Happy, satisfied employees work better. They are more committed, more willing to go the extra mile, so much more enjoyable to be around—to work with—than miserable ones.

> "I think Corning realizes that happy people tend to be more productive... it's a very human-centered corporation."
>
> MARC WHALEN AND LISA CHACON, RESEARCH SCIENTISTS
> CORNING INCORPORATED

After working 12 years as a nurse, Heather Munro found self-esteem and satisfaction as a production technician at KI (formerly Kreuger International), an office furniture factory. She says, "here, no one tells you what to do and everyone is equal." KI has been using a Japanese management style, according to Scott Deugo. It gives employees a common goal, a sense of worth and input into the company's decision making. KI focuses on teamwork, respect, trust and equality.

Listen to employees. Listening has so many benefits it's a wonder it isn't used more as a management strategy. In addition to being able to read the day-to-day company barometer via employees who work the floor—often they know more about what needs to be done than you do—listening to employees boosts their self-esteem. One of the leaders I spoke with related how she frequently sat with staff at their desks, chatting and listening to what they had to say. She said, "you can inspire feelings of trust—of willingness to share, in people, just by looking into their eyes and listening."

Sometimes all that is required is a nod of the head; sometimes just a few words can turn feelings of despair into feelings of accomplishment. My sister-in-law tells of a young salesman new to the job who was trying to sell hi-tech equipment to her lab, and although his efforts were substantial, his sales were not. His boss stopped at his desk for a moment, noticing that he was low, and asked how things were going. The salesman replied that despite his efforts he had not made a sale. The boss didn't offer suggestions or ideas, he just told the salesman that selling high priced technical equipment was not like selling knick-knacks. "It takes time," his boss said, "when we hired you we knew you were a good salesman and would do very well. Just keep up your effort and you will succeed." The salesman's self-esteem grew on the spot and eventually he did become the excellent salesman his boss told him he was that day.

Giving and receiving feedback is a leader's magic wand. Not only does giving effective feedback let your people know how they are doing in general, it lets them know how they are performing relative to the goals and standards that they are expected to meet. When they succeed, their sense of accomplishment soars. When they are less sucessful, provide positive feedback, perhaps with a peer coach or mentor, to help them to improve, to grow and to feel good about themselves.

Positive feedback belongs in public—negative feedback in private.

Schedule meetings to collect employee feedback as well. Encourage staff, in small groups, to come to meetings with suggestions about policies or procedures that need fixing, changing, updating. Ask staff to rank suggestions in order of priority, and together set up a plan for who is to do what, by when.

> "All you need to do is tell people they are no good ten times a day, and very soon they will believe it."
>
> LIN YUTANG, (1895-1976)
> AUTHOR AND TEACHER

Create an open and trusting atmosphere and you will be treated in a straightforward and truthful manner in return. Nothing demoralizes staff more than being kept in the dark about the state of the organization, or being lied to about their own situation.

A few years ago I read about the Open Book style of management, in which nothing was hidden from employees. Studies reported that productivity and personal achievement soared and turnover fell. Springfield Remanufacturing Corporation is one example of Open Book Management. Says Jack Stack, President and CEO, "every single one of our employees can see our profit and loss statements at all times. This shows people how they impact company profitability. Machinists who are responsible for 43¢ of productivity a minute know the cost of a ten-minute coffee break. A janitor who is responsible for buying supplies can see how the price he pays for things affects the bottom line. It's the employees' company. They decide whether we succeed or fail." This environment, because it ensures involvement, increases employee satisfaction and grows leaders.

Open Book Management is at the far end of full disclosure spectrum. If that is too far to the left, you can adopt a more conservative, but equally effective approach. About every six weeks Stuart Levine, former CEO of Dale Carnegie Training & Associates Inc., collected tapes from employees containing questions they would have liked Levine to answer. He replied and sent them back with an eye toward employee satisfaction, Levine also frequently surveyed his 3,500 + workers to find out what they thought about their work environment and to solicit any suggestions, concerns, issues they may have had. Their requests were implemented if at all possible.

4. Provide Rewards to Your Staff

Recognition and acknowledgement of a job well done, in addition to a competitive salary, is powerful. That's why, in terms of employee satisfaction Southwest Airlines ranks second in *Fortune*'s 2000 survey of "The 100 Best Companies to Work For in America." Positive employee comments echo through those Southwest aisles, "Working here is truly an unbelievable experience. They treat you with respect, pay you well and empower you. They use your ideas to solve problems. They encourage you to be yourself. I love going to work!"

"Compensation is a right. Recognition is a gift," said Rosabeth Moss Kanter, well-known researcher. How very true! In survey after survey workers today indicate that while they expect fair, competitive salaries, it is recognition that they really need and want. Dennis McCarthy, President of the Paradigm Marketing Group, a training company, put it quite emphatically. "One of the most powerful statements of commitment you can make is to let employees know when they've done a good job." Recognition takes many forms as it marches across the American workplace—but all who have implemented recognition programs agree that they build self-image, morale, camaraderie, a sense of satisfaction and productivity.

The "I Caught You Doing Something Right" program has been a big hit at Dale Carnegie since its inception. Every week one employee, nominated by co-workers, wins a $250 award for a job well done.

At Honeywell, a variety of recognition programs have been instituted to raise morale. Several times a year the "Chairman's Achievement Award" is presented based on individuals nominated by co-workers. Other Honeywell annual awards include recognition for great people managers, outstanding engineers and scientists, excellent technical service people. The list goes on—each award has a similar function: letting employees know that they are valued.

Ideally leaders should recognize employees every day for the things they do well—frequently verbal appreciation is sufficient to offer valuable recognition. Research shows, however, that leaders be they department heads, district managers or supervisors—don't give this recognition often enough.

Add these methods of showing appreciation and giving recognition—suggested to me by various leaders—to the ones you already use.

> "A lot of companies are offering compensation bonuses of some kind or another, but you know what? That's just money. It doesn't really keep your employees in the end."
>
> Jacqueline McDonald, Director, Human Resources
> Mintz & Partners

PRAISE EMPLOYEES OFTEN

Training and development experts advise
that in order to praise employees most effectively...

◆ Praise promptly—it's most effective when given immediately after a job well done.

◆ Praise sincerely—simply, from the heart.

◆ Praise precisely—let employees know specifically what they've done well.

◆ Praise without giving any criticism—don't mix.

◆ Praise face-to-face—tell employee directly... or

◆ Praise in front of someone else—this lets the employee know what they've done well and communicates to others that you noticed and appreciated what they did... or

◆ Praise to others when the employee isn't there—a most effective way to ensure that not only does the employee hear the accolades, but others are made aware of it and transmit it along.

RECOGNIZE EMPLOYEES

◆ Send a handwritten note—keep notes handy with stamped envelopes, ready to write, ready to send from anywhere.

◆ Host a breakfast—have managers cook and serve. Failing that, have it catered, so employees feel important.

◆ Host an afternoon tea or an ice cream social.

◆ Install a wall of fame—with photos and accomplishments of top-performing employees.

◆ Highlight top-performing employees on the company website, in the company newsletter or in a newspaper ad.

◆ Present framed certificates of achievement—at a special "Employee Appreciation Day" luncheon or dinner, or at a company meeting.

◆ Begin staff meetings by passing praise along—read a customer letter thanking an employee, relay a phone call or a conversation giving praise.

◆ Call an employee's extension at the end of the day and leave a voice mail message giving praise or appreciation. You can do the same by sending an e-mail.

◆ Pass praise along—provide a time or place, such as a newsletter, for one employee to praise another or celebrate the progress of a group project.

◆ Give a pat on the back. It is sometime all that is needed to demonstrate appreciation.

◆ Offer pairs of theatre or ballgame tickets.

◆ Provide dinner for two at a top-notch restaurant.

◆ Give a weekend get-away.

Looking through this list, an old friend reminded me of two things. *First,* remember to recognize an employee who has taken the initiative to attempt the "seemingly impossible" and while perhaps not succeeding, certainly has not failed. *Second,* institute recognition programs that encourage recognition, not discourage it by being unattainable.

> "The greater danger for most of us is not that our aim is too high and we miss it, but that it is too low and we reach it."
>
> ANONYMOUS

When a company needs assistance, rewarding employees for their help can easily become a win/win situation. Robert Rogers, CEO of Texas Industries asked his employees for ideas to save his cement and slag company. He got them—ideas that are responsible for 15% of TXI's profits. Rogers gave the employees who offered the suggestion group bonuses that can accrue to 20% of their salaries.

Gabar Szirmak, CEO of Informance Balance Inc. wanted to share company profits with employees who best exemplify core company values. He hosted a black tie dinner and awards ceremony during which he gave away $180,000 in bonus money. His "Academy Awards" categories included: teamwork, dedication, results and innovation. Management chose the nominees, while the entire staff voted on the winners. Actually everyone was a winner because the evening was special, fun and motivating.

Gordon Bethune, CEO of Continental Airlines had to improve the situation at the airline, or there would be no airline left to improve. Choosing what he thought was most important to passengers—arriving on time—he told employees that every month that Continental's "on time" percentage was good enough to make the top five nationwide (according to Department of Transportation figures) every employee would receive $65.

"Good bosses make their people think they have more ability than they have, so they consistently do better work than they thought they could."
CHARLES E. WILSON, FORMER PRESIDENT
GENERAL MOTORS

The rationale for this was that if customers won, employees won too. It worked so well that Continental raised the bar *and the reward*. Getting planes in on time became a central element of Continental's culture.

With so much competition in the marketplace and such a small talent pool from which to fish for super staff, everyone looks for ways to keep the best. Recognizing and rewarding employees provides them with one of their basic needs: self-fulfillment. Noticing and appreciating their accomplishments by rewarding them, keeps employees excited about their job and their company.

5. Provide a Supportive Community

That's why Martin Rosenblum works at Harley-Davidson. He discovered camaraderie, teamwork and a sense of accomplishment that made him feel he was a contributor. "For the first time in my life I feel like I'm part of a community. Harley is the university I've always been looking for."

Leaders must be coaches, guides and mentors to their people. To undertake this huge responsibility effectively they must demonstrate a sensitivity to the needs of their people—a task that often requires creative and innovative juggling. An outstanding leader I spoke with said her role was to create a looking glass that revealed to her whole organization what each individual part was doing. This, she said, was achieved through small meetings, talks over coffee, network building. The goal was to bring her people together. Another leader I spoke with commented that he felt he was responsible for ensuring that his staff felt they were treated with respect and dignity. He wanted them to feel that their ideas matter, that their recommendations have a chance of being implemented and that they have the opportunity to make a difference.

Even before a new employee arrives, begin getting the place ready so that the new recruit will feel comfortable and a part of the group. Create an environment that is conducive to each new recruit contributing their expertise and learning new skills, so eventually they have even more to contribute.

" A community is like a ship; everyone ought to be prepared to take the helm."
HENRIK IBSEN (1828-1906)
PLAYWRIGHT

Designate a peer to be the recruit's buddy for the first week. Responsibilities would include orienting, answering questions about procedures, introducing them to the rest of the staff, explaining basic day-to-day tasks and how the department connects to the overall company operations. Keep in mind this is not a coaching or mentoring role.

As the leader it is your responsibility to welcome new employees at the start of their first day, and meet with them later in the day to answer questions. Ask them what they did that day and what their impressions of the workflow were. Reiterate some of the important points made at the interview: company objectives, company standards, company expectations of new employees.

At the end of the first week, take time to meet again with the new recruit. Discuss how the week went, and encourage the new staffer to ask questions that may have arisen. This initial investment of time paves the way for effective mentoring and prevents serious problems later on.

"An outstanding leader clearly articulates the goals and objectives and makes sure every member of the organization understands the role he or she plays in achieving these goals..."
JACK BINGLEMAN, PRESIDENT
STAPLES INTERNATIONAL

MENTORING

One of the most effective means to ensure that your business environment is a supportive, "glad-to-be-here" environment is mentoring.

> "What I find consistently with clients is that they're doing wonderful work in recruiting and working hard to be an employer of choice. But they're not putting the back door in place, which is retention."
>
> KATHY HERTIES, MANAGER, HUMAN RESOURCES
> KPMG LLP

Mentors have an important role and therefore must be selected with care. Experienced managers who are confident in themselves, able to park their egos, and see mentoring as a process for the good of the employee and the company alike, make the best mentors—and can be successfully paired with a new recruit.

One final layer of mentoring can be added to those already mentioned—that of a "shadow mentor." Typically an experienced mentor, a shadow mentor meets occasionally with both mentor and employee to assess the relationship, resolve any issues that may have developed, and help all involved to keep preset goals at the forefront of their actions.

> "In a command and control organization, people protect knowledge because it is their claim to distinction."
>
> ROBERT HAAS, CEO
> LEVI STRAUSS & CO

Without doubt mentors share information, but for an organization to classify as a supportive community there must be the willingness of everyone to share. Jealously guarding information, rationalizing its safekeeping because "if I share what I know, I'm not going to be of value any more" is the quick route to corporate dwarfism. Integrating new staff, coaching them, sharing information, experience and knowledge on the other hand, is the quick route to corporate good health and long term growth.

MENTORING BENEFITS

Benefits are major—long lasting and include:

◆ Skilled training, especially in today's environment, where "new" is "old" in a flash. Mentors assist employees to keep learning.

◆ Increased productivity—since employees acquire new and better skills.

◆ An improvement cycle—as employees feel leaders are responsive to them, they respond in turn. In the end the organization improves.

◆ Employees quickly feel enfranchised.

MENTORING HOW-TO'S

◆ Devise a plan that best suits your corporate culture and management goals.

◆ Put a top-line manager in charge of mentoring.

◆ Choose mentors who are flexible, curious, adventurous—ones who will admit to ignorance.

◆ Train mentors. Many human resource consulting firms and employee training organizations offer training.

◆ Match mentors to employees by matching skills acquired to skills required.

◆ Match work schedules to facilitate easy contact between mentors and employees.

◆ Allow mentors and employees to be mentored to set their own schedules for meetings (frequency, location, length, etc.).

6. Provide a Balanced Work Environment

More than ever before, today's workforce is looking for balance. The recent National Study of Changing Workforce by the Families and Work Institute found that 60% of those interviewed felt the effect on their personal/family life was a very important determinant in deciding whether to take their current job.

Business Week's second survey on family and work found that only 49% of those surveyed felt that they could have a decent family life and still get ahead at work. The ranks of the discontented included not just working mothers, but also childless couples and singles. Men expressed greater frustration than women—and the unhappiest of all were employees responsible for elder care at home.

A new study by the Conference Board of Canada shows no more than 10% of companies offer employees any emergency or elder care case management assistance. Front line managers may also be caught off balance. Pressure from supervisors to improve performance, produce better results and keep costs in line vie with employee demands to cut back *their* hours to help balance *their* lives. These managers end up squeezed from both sides. The study found that only one third of

> **"It is not clear that anyone—employees, employer, community agencies or government—is prepared for the substantial impact that growing elder care responsibilities will have on the labor force in coming years."**
> THE 1997 NATIONAL STUDY OF THE CHANGING WORKFORCE

> **"20% of working parents are of the 'sandwich generation'—raising children and caring for elderly relatives."**
> THE 1997 NATIONAL STUDY OF THE CHANGING WORKFORCE

> **"More than one-third of employees with elder care responsibilities in the past year, reduced work hours or took time off to provide that care."**
> THE 1997 NATIONAL STUDY OF THE CHANGING WORKFORCE

> **"Only one in four employees has access to elder care resources and referral services through their employer."**
> THE 1997 NATIONAL STUDY OF THE CHANGING WORKFORCE

organizations offer managers support to handle these work-life balancing issues, while less than one quarter recognize and reward supportive managers.

It appears that strategies for juggling work and family in many instances, are not working very well. In many companies strategies to lessen this employee discontent, has never even been considered. Statistics such as these require today's leaders to take note and make changes.

Achieving a healthy balance between work and family is why Reem Samra works at Deloitte & Touche. After the birth of her second child she wanted to cut back her hours, but didn't want to jeopardize her chance of making partner. "Human resources people have come to me and convinced me that I could work fewer hours and still be in line for a partnership."

Samra's schedule is now 15% lighter and she points out, "this isn't just about 'mommies,' Generation Xers care about balance too. A young manager in my department is working reduced hours, and he doesn't have kids. He does, however, have a life."

"It's important to have flexibility over a life span or a career span. There has to be a deeper level of personal satisfaction, a sense that things are all right. If you can help people find that level, they tend to stick around."

DOUG BURGUM, CHAIRMAN & CEO
GREAT PLAINS SOFTWARE

"On average U.S. companies lose half their employees in four years."

FREDERICK REICHHELD, MANAGEMENT CONSULTANT
BAIN & CO.

"Balance is not about taking off the day when your kids get sick. Balance is what's needed when your kids are playing in a softball tournament, and they really want you to be there... There's a huge amount of value in giving people the opportunity to say yes to things that are important to them but may conflict with their regular working hours."

DOUG BURGUM, CHAIRMAN & CEO
GREAT PLAINS SOFTWARE

AN UNBALANCED WORK ENVIRONMENT IS A HAZARD:

◆ Constant work overload—"too much work, too little time"—is often the standard in today's business, however, when it is relentless, employees feel overwhelmed by an unmanageable load and both their productivity and their attitude are negatively affected.

◆ Inadequate control of work environment—employees want to "own" their job, determine their priorities, have some autonomy in their approach, be able to make some decisions. Withholding this autonomy results in frustration and lack of balance.

◆ Insufficient rewards—employees look for both financial rewards and non-financial benefits. Lack of balance is certainly the result when rewards are minimized or compromised.

◆ Disintegration of community environment—community is one of the most powerful needs of employees, removing it can be devastating.

◆ Lack of open-mindedness—many of today's workplaces breed fear and mistrust because of their secretive and uncommunicative natures. In such a closed environment, employees come away feeling they have been treated unfairly, and as a result lack loyalty.

◆ Contradictory values—employees quickly become suspicious when companies say one thing, but do another.

Incorporate these strategies into your company's operating action plan to stay balanced.

Keep in mind that like everything else in life "the balance" changes. It is not a firmly cemented teeter-totter. Be prepared to continue to make changes so the lives of your employees and your company remain balanced.

"A great company is where you want to end up and spend most of your life. Most of life is a search for people and institutions worthy of your loyalty and commitment. People yearn for that."

FREDERICK REICHHELD, MANAGEMENT CONSULTANT BAIN & CO.

STRATEGIES TO ASSIST YOUR COMPANY'S ACTION PLAN STAY BALANCED

◆ Communicate.

1. Talk to employees.
2. Ask questions.
3. Use a variety of opportunities to find out what is going on.
4. Have regularly scheduled meetings.
5. Engage in one-on-one discussions.
6. Utilize small informal groups.
7. Use a variety of means to get your message out to employees: e-mails, memos, retreats, newsletters, updating bulletins.

◆ Identify specific problem areas.

◆ Detail specific improvements to be made.

◆ Involve employees in the search for the most appropriate solutions.

◆ Implement—take notes on effectiveness, results.

◆ Get feedback and make changes—check that solutions are indeed effective and implementable.

7. Provide Inspiring, Motivating Leadership

Inspire your people by providing them with answers to important questions such as these: Why are we here? Who are we as a company? What are we doing that is important enough for us to be spending the days of our lives here?

Your reply must make a convincing case for working with you—clearly explaining why the company is important, why its products and services are beneficial and how they make a positive difference in customers' lives.

Ben Zander, conductor of the Boston Philharmonic Orchestra has an excellent method to get the most from the students he teaches at the New England Conservatory of Music. His idea, when applied to business, could have phenomenal results. "Every fall on the first day of class, I make an announcement: 'Everyone gets an A!' There's only one condition. Students have to submit a letter—written on that first day but dated the following May that begins: 'Dear Mr. Zander, I got my A because…' In other words, they have to tell me at the beginning of their course, who they will have become by the end of the course that will justify this extraordinary grade. That simple 'A' changes everything. It transforms my relationship with everybody in the room. As leaders, we're giving out grades in every encounter we have with people. We can choose to give out grades as an expectation to live up to, and that we can reassess them according to performance. Or we can offer grades as a possibility to live into. The second approach is much more powerful." A great leader sees his people not only as they are, but as they can grow to be.

The characteristics of inspiring, motivating leadership are as variable as today's organizations. What the employees of one organization find inspiring, employees of the next may find too eccentric or too staid. Leaders I spoke to all agree that inspiring, motivating leadership requires an internal fire, a passion that is transmitted to every corner of the organization—

making everyone with whom it comes in contact, passionate as well. The CEO of Cisco Systems, Inc., John Chambers, inspires with his egalitarian attitude. He treats his people like peers—asking advice, giving over power and resources and keeping them challenged. Tom Stemberg, CEO and Chairman of the Board of Staples inspires with his hands-on approach to running the company—by doing everything from visiting competitors' stores and his own, to delivering goods to customers. He has passed on to his people the passion that grows when you discover a new and better way to take care of business.

Both have been hugely successful, because their people have taken up the cause of their respective leaders and would take that passion to the ends of the earth if necessary.

Passion is an incredibly powerful motivator. Its power lies in its ability to encourage those imbued to go the extra mile—to look for another possibility—to make the effort one more time. Zeal compels action.

It's contagious, says Ross Lederer of Craft-Bilt Manufacturing Co., "it must emanate from every part of your being. Whether it is passion for country, company, parenthood, or something as mundane as baking a loaf of bread, wear your passion on your shirt sleeve. Famous and infamous leaders throughout history have moved the masses with their passion."

Passionate leaders are a tremendous energy source—powering their people to perform at higher levels—lighting up the organization with their enthusiasm.

Do you inspire your people? Would they go to the ends of the earth for you?

Projections estimated that by the year 2008, there will be about 161 million jobs for 155 million workers. Inspirational leadership will assist in motivating employees to join *you*.

SEVEN WAYS TO INSPIRE:

1. Look for opportunities to inspire. Be innovative. Experiment. Take risks. Stretch the boundaries.

2. Share your vision. Take your passion to your people. As you transmit the belief you have in the cause, you will be able to enlist others in it.

3. Be unimpeachable and compassionate. Be above reproach, but be understanding so others can follow with confidence.

4. Be an enabler. Once you've transmitted your ideas, your goals, allow others to act on them—carry them forward.

5. Recognize others for what they are. Expect high performance—but don't expect the sun, the moon and the stars.

6. Walk the talk. Be what you want others to be.

7. Recognize changes. Celebrate achievements. Recognition reinforces your goals and strengthens the collective passion and drive.

To provide inspirational leadership requires two conditions be present. First, you must be inspired yourself and, second, you must know your people so well that you know what will inspire them.

Providing motivational leadership can move mountains. It carries you and your people forward, simply because it inspires a bigger, better response. It can certainly encourage you to work for you—and others to work for you as well.

"Whether it be so-called disenfranchised youth, overpaid job-hoppers, or cynical and aging middle management, the challenge to motivate others has never been more difficult."

CHRIS DAVIS, NATIONAL MANAGER, BRAND DEVELOPMENT
SEARS HOME CENTRAL

An old fable bears this out. Once long ago, in a land far away, a wanderer came upon a laborer, who was angrily pounding away at a stone. "What are you doing?" asked the young man. "I'm trying to shape this stone, and it's back-breaking work." As the young man continued on his journey, he came upon another stoneworker. "What are you doing?" he asked. "I'm shaping stones for a building," this stoneworker replied, matter-of-factly. Before long, he came upon a third worker, who was singing as he chipped away at the stone. The young man asked him what he was doing and the stone mason smiled and replied, "I'm building a cathedral."

Would you work for you?　　　　　Yes ☐　　No ☐　　I'm not sure at this time ☐

SOME TOUGH QUESTIONS

These questions are real "look-at-yourself-in-the-mirror" questions. They require not only real and truthful answers—they demand action.

1. **What motivates your people to do their best job? What satisfies them? What satisfiers do you provide?**

_____

_____

_____

2. **What training do you provide? Is it consistent? Regular? Professional? How many hours in a year are devoted to professional training? (Compare yourself to *Fortune*'s 100 Best Companies to Work For).**

_____

_____

_____

3. What measures have you instituted to empower your people? Do they feel empowered? Do they act empowered? What else could you do?

_____

_____

_____

4. What makes your organization one of the best to work for? What could you implement that would make it even better?

_____

_____

_____

_____

5. How is feedback provided? How often? How honest is the feedback that is generated? How constructive is it?

_____

_____

_____

_____

6. How do you reward your people? Do these rewards satisfy them? What other rewards could you enact tomorrow?

_____

_____

_____

_____

7. My wife still remembers her first job, as does one of my sons.
    In both instances they were shown which cubicle was theirs and
    just told "to do it." How do you integrate new staff into your
    organization? How do you ensure they have the necessary tools to
    do the job?

    _____

    _____

    _____

8. Who performs the role of mentor in your organization? How good
    are they at it? Is it beneficial? What would improve your mentoring
    program?

    _____

    _____

    _____

9. So much coverage is given to stress and balance in the workplace.
    What are you doing to create a balance between work and home?
    What are you doing to alleviate stress? What else could you do?

    _____

    _____

    _____

10. Are you providing inspiring, motivating leadership to yourself?
    To others? How?

    _____

    _____

    _____

Chapter 4

Taking Care Of Business

Would You Work for You?
*Yes, if Only... **You Know the Skills to Do the Job***

No matter how well you know yourself and your people, to be an outstanding leader you must also recognize the specific prerequisites of outstanding leadership—the skills needed to encourage you to work for yourself—the capabilities required to encourage someone else to work for you. When I asked leaders to outline specific skills they felt were essential to do the job, these six were repeatedly mentioned:

♦ Hiring

♦ Team Building

♦ Managing Time

♦ Delegating

♦ Resolving Conflict

♦ Making Decisions

How do they rate on your list of priorities?

"The three most important skills an effective leader must have would be: first to know yourself—both strengths and weaknesses. Only then can you know whom to ask for advice to complement your own insights. Second, to build a team that complements your strengths (rather than mimics them) and that, as a whole, has the diversity, style and breadth of expertise to effectively tackle the strategic challenges faced by the organization. And third, motivate people to drive the organization in the direction you have chosen by giving them training, responsibility and ultimately accountability."

R.F. Conlin, Vice President, Marketing
General Motors of Canada Limited

HIRING

This is now a much more complicated process than in years past. The attitudes of "how cheaply can I find someone" or "if it doesn't work out I'll find someone else" have been replaced with "who will help me grow my company." The revolving "hire-fire" door is costly and counterproductive.

In an interview with the *American Compensation Association Journal*, in the winter of '95, Herb Kelleher, Chairman, President and CEO indicated that Southwest Airlines maintained its corporate culture through its hiring practices. "We are zealous about hiring... we are looking for attitudes that are positive... we want folks who have a good sense of humor and people who are interested in performing as a team and take joy in team results instead of individual accomplishments. If you start with the type of person you want to hire presumably you can build a workforce that is prepared for the culture you desire..." In a 1999 interview with *Chief Executive*, he seemed to continue where he had left off, "We try to value each person individually at Southwest and to be cognizant of them as human beings—not just people who work for our company. We try to memorialize and celebrate and sympathize with and commemorate the things that happen to them in their personal lives. What we're really trying to say is, 'we value you as people apart from the fact that you work here.' "

Interesting and effective hiring techniques have surfaced in recent years. Cisco Systems, Inc. looks to hire not by using the conventional help wanted ads, but by waving placards that read www.cisco.com/jobs during football games, or by manning an information booth at the Santa Clara Home and Garden Show. It has to do with demographics they say. For example, Michael McNeal, when he was Director of Corporate Development at Cisco, thought that anyone who can afford a home in Santa Clara—let alone a garden—has to be at the top of their profession. Statistics seem to verify McNeal's observation. Of the 50,000 people who attended the show that year 78% held professional degrees and worked in the hi-tech sector. The Home and Garden Show attracts exactly the kind of person Cisco *wants to hire*.

Other effective recruitment strategies include asking current staff who they know that would make good hires, and partnering with other companies to sponsor job fairs. The thinking behind sharing the spotlight with other similar companies is that potential hires might be reluctant to go to a recruitment session for only one prospective employer, whereas such opportunities seem more attractive when there are several companies to consider.

Posting jobs online, while not new to techies, has been gaining acceptance in the general marketplace. Forrester Research predicts that by 2001 most companies will be searching on the Internet for candidates. The Net is advantageous because it permits a worldwide search easily and initial interviews can be conducted by e-mail. Many websites contain databases of resumes—albeit most charge for use. By keying in search parameters such as job titles, particular industries and city names, your search is narrowed down. With Internet portals such as AOL and Yahoo you can also place your own job requirements. Write your ad carefully, being specific so you won't be inundated with inappropriate replies. It might also be useful and forward thinking to add a career page to your website. Prospective candidates can see what positions are available while they get a glimpse of your organization. Don't however, give up the face-to-face interview—it's still essential to determine the candidate's soft skills.

Some leaders remarked that no matter the specific hiring strategy, it makes good sense (and dollars too) to quantify results of your search techniques, to determine how much each recruiting event costs, how many contacts it yields, and how many of those result in interviews and successful hires.

Several of the HR consultants I spoke with commented that rarely do companies do their homework *before* they begin the hiring process. Rarely do companies carefully consider in advance, the skills a new hire should have and whether those skills should be different from the ones the current occupant of the position holds. They seldom ask themselves if the new hire is right for this job. They seldom think through what they themselves need. Consequently, the result becomes a lopsided, inaccurate decision.

The challenge in hiring is to determine whether the person under consideration has the appropriate competencies required for the job—and whether once hired, they are ready and willing to be further trained. It is also important when hiring to assure that the goals of the company are aligned with those of the prospective employee. One way to do this is by having the candidate prepare a business plan covering their anticipated area of involvement in the organization. Assessing whether the candidate's plan and your vision are aligned, effectively checks their probable fit within the organization.

Consultants offered several additional suggestions to avoid the pitfalls inherent in the hiring challenge.

> "Some people can almost become professional interviewees. They can impress any potential employer, but that doesn't mean they're the best candidate."
>
> WILLI WIESNER, ASSOCIATE PROFESSOR OF HUMAN RESOURCE MANAGEMENT MCMASTER UNIVERSITY

♦ Never hire just to fill a vacancy. The time and money you will spend to correct the error just doesn't pay.

♦ Experience is an important evaluator. However, too much emphasis on experience can eliminate from consideration valuable candidates with experience in other fields. Alternatively it can emphasize length of tenure, rather than duration of success.

♦ Education, while certainly a valid criteria

to screen for, doesn't indicate whether the applicant has a positive attitude, or has any of the "soft skills," including empathy and flexibility, that are so necessary and sought after today.

◆ Mirror-image hiring is perhaps a natural reaction. However hiring those with whom we have a great deal in common is bound to create an uneven workforce. Remember your strengths, but heed your weaknesses as well. Also bear in mind that holding unrealistic expectations of the candidate—such as looking for a miracle worker—can only lead to disappointment for all concerned.

◆ Don't believe everything you see or hear. Create a way to check the credibility of the glowing descriptions you are told by candidates or their references.

◆ Give references the opportunity to just talk about the candidate. When speaking to the references, outline the specific job you are looking to fill and then probe to see how the applicant might fit the job. Questions such as, "What parameters might be changed to help the candidate succeed in the job?" "Does the candidate have some abilities that can be strengthened with training?" would be appropriate.

◆ Don't rely only on references supplied by the prospective employee. How often have you heard about recommendations that indicated brilliance, only to discover the applicant didn't even have a 15-watt glow? It has been rumored that excellent recommendations have been given by former employers just to get rid of troublesome employees. The best reference is often someone you know who has worked with the candidate and can give you the straight goods.

◆ Ignoring "soft skills" because they are so hard to define is common. Be clear about what "soft skills" are required, based on the situations the candidate will face on the job. Decide who is needed—a bridge builder, a strong communicator, a marketer, or someone conversant in working with a wide variety of divisions—and look for a canddate who possesses those skills.

♦ Pencil-and-paper psychological tests offer an additional assessment tool to assist in determining personality. Many of the tests consist of a series of questions such as, "Do you like to work alone?" or "Are you happier when working alone?" or "Do you enjoy working in a group?" The candidate can indicate their answer on a scale, such as *always, often, infrequently* or *never.* Results can be compared to established norms for the personality characteristics being sought. With so many tests available on the market that evaluate many different desirable qualities, a leader may need assistance in determining the most appropriate test. This form of assessment, however, may be a useful one to consider.

♦ Listening between the lines during an interview results in a much more complete picture than can be gleaned just from asking standard questions. Candidates are often effusive about what they do well, but silent about capabilities which they don't possess. Look between the lines of the resumé. Ask "between the lines" questions during the interview such as "I don't see June '97 - August '98 referred to on your resumé, what were you doing then?"

♦ Being able and willing to learn and grow from past experiences is a characteristic common to many successful professionals. It there-fore makes sense to locate individuals who possess these qualities right at the start of the hiring process. While this is not a simple task, there are questions designed to investigate an applicant's ability to learn new behaviors from experience.

AN APPLICANT'S ASSESSMENT QUESTIONNAIRE

To determine an applicant's ability to learn new behaviors from previous experience ask questions such as:

◆ What was your most challenging job? Why?
  What did you learn from this job?

◆ What was your least challenging job? Why?
  What did you learn from this job?

◆ In what situation did you find that you had to overcome major obstacles to meet your objectives? What did you do? Why?
  What did you learn from this experience?

◆ Who do you admire most? Who do you admire least? Why?

◆ In what situation did you attempt to do something, but failed?
  Why did you fail? What did you learn from this situation?

◆ Describe a bad experience that you had.
  What did you learn from it?

◆ Describe a situation where you tried to help someone change.
  What strategy did you use? How did the situation end?

◆ Describe a mistake you made in dealing with people.
  What did you learn from it?

◆ What was your best learning experience? What was your worst learning experience? What did you learn from each of them?

◆ Describe the last major change you made. Why did you do it?
  How did it work out? What did you learn from making this change?

Evaluate each candidate's answers on a scale of one to five, using the following seven criteria:

- *generalization* - weaker candidates have a tendency to generalize their experience, not being able to draw out specifically what they learned in a given situation or why. Stronger candidates are much more specific.

- *the learning experience* - weaker candidates tend toward extremes, either expected answers or exaggerated ones. They have difficulty explaining specifically what they learned. Stronger candidates are more open about their mistakes, about their weaknesses. They may be tough on themselves but are eager to discuss their response.

- *the long view* – weaker candidates have a simpler view of people and their jobs with fewer layers of understanding. Stronger candidates describe situations and events with more significant depth of analysis.

- *the "why"* – weaker candidates tend to focus more on "what" happened and less on "why" it happened. They have difficulty expressing whether any learning took place and what that learning was. Stronger candidates consider the "why" more than the "what" and are not hesitant to explain what was learned and what they would do differently next time.

- *focus of interest* – weaker candidates are more concerned with the incidentals of the job—chance of promotion, fringe benefits, etc. Stronger candidates are more interested in the content of the job and their future in it.

- *ability to analyze* – weaker candidates are able to analyze failure, but are more reluctant to acknowledge their role in it. Stronger candidates are also able to analyze failure and success and admit their role in both.

- *self-awareness* – weaker candidates are not accurately self-aware—overstating strengths, trying inconsistently to correct weaknesses and not accurately judging their limits. Stronger candidates are more accurately aware of strengths, weaknesses and limits.

	Generalize/Particularize	Learning Experience	The Long View	What or Why	Focus of Interest	Ability to Analyze	Self Aware	Total
Candidate: _____ Date: _____ Score each question for the seven criteria indicated on a scale of 1 to 5 (5 being strong)								
1 What was your most challenging job? Why? What did you learn from this job?								
2 What was your least challenging job? Why? What did you learn from this job?								
3 In what situation did you find that you had to overcome major obstacles to meet your objectives? What did you do? Why? What did you learn from this experience?								
4 Who do you admire most? Who do you admire least? Why?								
5 In what situation did you attempt to do something, but failed? Why did you fail? What did you learn from this situation?								
6 Describe a bad experience that you had. What did you learn from it?								
7 Describe a situation where you tried to help someone change. What strategy did you use? How did the situation end?								
8 Describe a mistake you made in dealing with people. What did you learn from it?								
9 What was your best learning experience? What was your worst learning experience? What did you learn from each of them?								
10 Describe the last major change you made. Why did you do it? How did it work out? What did you learn from making it?								

By utilizing an interview analysis such as the one on the previous page, you will be able to interview more effectively—and therefore hire the right person for the right job. Jeff Bezos, Founder and CEO of Amazon.com Inc. believes that his company's success is the result of constantly improving his workforce and raising the entry-level standards.

Recently, alternative techniques to traditional one-on-one interviews have surfaced. Of particular interest is the interview conducted not only by the manager/leader, but also by the group with whom the interviewee will be working. Following the interview, the group meets to share their impressions of the candidate's strengths and weaknesses. This format, while it may have a tendency to be intimidating, is nonetheless valuable if the candidate is to be working in a group.

A behavioral component has recently been added to the arsenal of interview techniques. Candidates are questioned about what they would do in hypothetical situations or how they acted in a particular situation in the past. For example, instead of asking "Are you good with difficult clients?" an interviewer would say, "Give me an example of a situation with a difficult client—and tell me how you dealt with it." The next question would be, "Why did you decide to do that?" This technique expands the parameters of the interview to include justification and examples of the "why" not just the "what."

When all is said and done, ensure you present the new recruit with clearly defined expectations, in writing. This includes a job description and longer term goals, as well as "promises" and "guarantees" made by both parties. Put a signed copy in the employee's file and give another signed copy to them.

Knowing what you know, would you hire you to work for you?

TEAM BUILDING

Employees are individuals. They can contribute as individuals or as members of a team.
While there are situations where individual
effort is necessary or preferred, in many,

"All of us are smarter than any one of us."

CHARLIE P. CROCKETT, SALES DIRECTOR,
AUTOMOTIVE AFTERMARKET DIVISION
3M

indeed, in most workplace situations today, teamwork is the model of
choice. Many workplace studies confirm that when people work in teams,
more is accomplished—and the quality of that work is improved.

As a leader interested in increasing your organization's productivity,
facilitating the building of teams is certainly a skill to master and maintain.

THE BASIC REQUIREMENTS FOR A SUCCESSFUL TEAM

◆ A work environment that facilitates rather than discourages the
interaction of team members. A central, open space does that.
Rows of small one-person cubicles does not.

◆ Communications technology that encourages quick, open
communication. Accessibility to intranet, e-mail, networked
computer systems, conference call equipment to start.

◆ Common goals and objectives that are clearly understood
and accepted by all team members.

◆ Access to needed information so everyone knows what they're doing
now, why they're doing it and what they'll be doing in the future.

◆ Reinforcement of the value and significance of the work they
are doing and how this work is for the good of the entire
organization and its customers.

◆ To be connected to each other in cyberspace and in real space.

CREATING A TEAM

A client of mine, Robert Minto Jr., CEO of the Attorneys Liability Protections Society (ALPS) wanted to make his organization feel, once again, "like a small company where all the key players maintain personal relationships with the customer. That relationship set us apart from the rest of the industry and remained the key to our incredible customer loyalty." As ALPS grew it developed departments that created distance between the company and its customers. Minto realized that if ALPS was to retain its unique flavor, it needed to change. After much research he planned to replace the existing organizational structure with multidisciplinary self-governing teams including no more than eleven members in a team. His idea was not a big hit.

One Friday, without prior warning, he called everyone together and divided the Underwriters, Claims, Marketing and Risk Management people into teams. "I knew I was creating chaos, but I knew I needed to move decisively or it would not happen." He was met with opposition, complaints and frustration. After several months Minto felt that enough of the old had crumbled and it was time to begin the process of teambuilding. He gave me a call. Together with all his staff we spent three days at a retreat—clearing the air and working to build the foundation for a "new ALPS"—a truly team-based organization, where people are empowered and enthusiastic.

The company is now growing at a rate that was inconceivable before teams. Minto says that at ALPS "change is now embraced rather than feared and new ideas flow from and in every direction." He recognizes that "a CEO needs to take risks sometimes, but they should be thoughtful and based on a clear view of the company's history and a sound concept for its future."

The ALPS message seems to be that there is no single way to get to teams, but early staff "buy in" and team building is necessary *if you want the teams to work for you.*

Generally a team can be expected to pass through four stages; first—*getting-to-know-you stage*; second—*trying-to-test-you stage*; third—*fitting-in-with-you stage*; and fourth—*working-comfortably-with-you stage*.

If you are building a team from inception it becomes your responsibility as a leader to facilitate through all four stages.

In the initial stage, help team members get to know each other to:

♦ clarify the team's purpose and goals;

♦ ensure team members are all included in growing the new relationship, their individual roles in it, and how the work will be divided and accomplished;

♦ provide basic information the team members need to begin the project—in writing;

♦ ask members to submit any questions they might have.

"A leader must be able to maximize team effectiveness... by selecting the right talent and then being able to create team confidence and enthusiasm."

JOHN ECCLESTON, DIRECTOR OF TRAINING
McDONALD'S RESTAURANTS OF CANADA LTD.

"Leadership has a harder job to do than just choose sides. It must bring sides together."

REV. JESSE JACKSON
CLERGYMAN, DIPLOMAT AND POLITICIAN

At the second stage, your involvement is slightly different. You become referee, guide and facilitator to:

♦ ensure that power and authority is satisfactorily agreed upon by group members; ensure every one has the opportunity to contribute;

♦ initiate decision-making parameters, much like a mother bird as it encourages her young out of the nest.

"The new leader is a facilitator, not an order giver."

JOHN NAISBITT, CHAIRMAN
NAISBITT GROUP

At the third stage take a step back, but remain in sight to:

♦ recognize and encourage team members' understanding
  and respect of each other;

♦ make use of team members' capabilities, their experience and skills;

♦ assist members to work together for the good of the group;

♦ assist to foster the attitude of "good of the group,"
  "power of the group," a "groupness."

*At the fourth stage your role moves to the sidelines. You become a coach and
information provider to:*

♦ maintain awareness of new procedures and methods and
  disseminate information to the group;

♦ facilitate the group's managing of the on-going change process;

♦ monitor progress and celebrate accomplishments;

♦ show support for the group. Tout the group throughout the organization.

At all stages:

♦ Give feedback that is immediate, positive, specific, related to
  performance and clear.

♦ Reinforce positive group performance immediately, frequently,
  specifically. Never reinforce and punish or criticize at the same time.

♦ Use team building strategies to:

  - celebrate and reward performance;

  - organize and redesign work to fit group performance;

- create goals not attainable without the group;

- develop communication systems that facilitate and encourage teamwork;

- develop operation systems that facilitate and encourage teamwork.

◆ Encourage "teamness" to:

- support and reward group co-operation instead of competition;

- pounce on and eradicate gossip;

- recognize the team, as a team.

◆ Support a Team Members' Bill of Rights which includes the right to:

- feedback – acknowledgement of contribution;

- sufficient and appropriate training to do the job;

- self-sufficiency;

- work in a comfortable, respectful environment;

- be heard;

- be respected as a person and a team member;

- honest, open communications.

◆ Rethink the compensation system:

- tie pay raises to learning skills needed by the team;

- give one-time bonuses for developing new skills.

◆ Change performance assessments:

 - from a focus on individuals to a focus on the team.

◆ Set specific challenges—and goals:

 - provide team building opportunities through group communication and dispute resolution;

 - assist with achieving goals if team gets bogged down.

◆ Keep the team small:

 - the optimum size for an effective team is four to nine people; no team should exceed thirty members.

◆ Keep the team evolving:

 - encourage growth and movement;

 - discourage stagnation.

One important aspect of team building is tolerance and a recognition of cultural differences between people. Research from the Center for Creative Leadership concurred with other similar studies noting that "respect for differences in people" is one of the most important qualities of a successful leader. It is strongly believed that understanding other cultures not only makes good business sense, but is the key to successful team building. Appreciating cultural diversity includes such minor issues as gift giving and receiving, the signs of personal greetings and the issues of timeliness—as well as such major issues as the significance of ethnicity and religion to a particular society and a fundamental understanding of the tenets and belief system of that society. Leaders who effectively understand, appreciate and motivate colleagues of many cultures and countries are valuable team builders.

You know you have a great team in your organization when its members help each other on their own, even though such assistance is not part of their responsibility.

You know you have a great team when everyone has a shared understanding of what your organization as a whole is trying to accomplish.

You know you have a great team when everyone knows the team values and how those values are used to make decisions.

> "...It's about listening to people—their problems and their aspirations. It's amazing how unaware you can be of the impact you have on people different from you. It's very easy for people to start feeling excluded because of artificial barriers."
>
> DENNIS LONGSTREET, PRESIDENT
> ORTHO BIOTECH

You know you have a great team when everyone's value in the organization is focused on teamwork, participation, innovation and quality.

Chris Higgins used team leadership experience gained in the Army Rangers to effectively lead a BankAmerica team that was required to develop a system which would enable the bank to accept deposits across state boundaries. His strategies for success included careful planning at the start—and lots of testing and refining at the end. He says, "my approach is 50% planning, 25% doing and 25% testing and training." He also advises, based on his military experiences, that different projects have much in common and while teams often face singular challenges, not every challenge requires a new plan of operation. Focusing on common elements between projects saves valuable resources and even more valuable time. Finally he is quick to remind project leaders that their job is not just solving problems and meeting objectives, it is also about maintaining momentum and morale. He ensures that each of his projects includes celebrations along the way, to mark the achievements of team members.

MANAGING TIME

Time is all you have. It can't be retrieved. It's irreplaceable. Use it well. Master time and you master your life.

Effective time management begins with planning. Create a prioritized "to do" list that outlines short term, mid-term and long-term projects, "must do's," goals and objectives. Experts in time management warn against two dangers regarding this planning stage. First, don't permit the planning process to become all-consuming. Obsessive list makers and time rearrangers may be left with too little time to act on their intentions. Second, be flexible enough to reprioritize as the situation changes. And it does—all the time!

My own piece of planning advice is to create a list in the format that best suits you. In our technological society, palm pilots have become *de rigeur* for maintaining lists. I use one. My youngest son keeps his list on his *Now-Up-to-Date* software program. My daughter keeps her list in an "old-fashioned" day-timer. It doesn't need to be a hi-tech solution, it needs to be a high-effective solution.

When prioritizing your time, experts agree there are three types of time to be blocked out.

- ◆ *internal time*—the optimum time to do your own work —*uninterrupted.* This is the time you are most productive on your own. For me, it's early in the morning, before the phones start ringing and the noises of the day distract. Find the best time for you and block it off.

- ◆ *external time*—the best time to hold meetings, hold conference calls, attend to the outside issues of the day. This is harder to block off because schedules need to be coordinated, but start with the time that works best for you and go from there. Whenever it's possible,

I suggest mid-morning or mid-afternoon for my external time, before another, less personally effective time is suggested by someone else.

◆   *self time*—the most important segment of time, yet the hardest time to block off and probably the least taken. Now that psychologists and HR people are validating its importance, blocking off time for your self has become more accepted and is less regarded as loafing on the job. A very few minutes of relaxation, introspection and head-clearing can do wonders to revive the mind, refresh the spirit and speed you on your way. You owe it to yourself, your staff and your associates to block off this time.

As you prioritize your work for the day—week—year, keep in mind Pareto's 80/20 principle, which states that if all work were arranged in order of value, 80% of value would come from 20% of work. It is your mandate to find the 20% of work that will yield 80% of value. Make that your first priority. Don't get bogged down with low value projects. Utilizing this principle could save a great deal of time, as you become comfortable delegating the 80% of work that only gives 20% of value.

"Don't say you don't have enough time. You have exactly the same number of hours per day that were given to Louis Pasteur, Michelangelo, Mother Teresa, Helen Keller, Leonardo da Vinci, Thomas Jefferson and Albert Einstein."

LIFE'S LITTLE INSTRUCTION CALENDAR

Another time management tactic I have found helpful not only in my business life but in my personal one as well, is to ask myself "what is the best use of my time right now?" This encourages me to stop for a minute, consider my priorities, my time constraints, my needs and the needs of those around me. Answering this question helps me get back on track when I'm distracted, or sluggish or torn between several demands.

During my discussions with leaders across the country, I asked what time problems they encounter most frequently.

THESE ARE THEIR TOP FIVE TIME-ROBBERS:

(i) Interruptions

It doesn't matter much whether they are caused by peers, by employees, by themselves or by technology. Interruptions are unscheduled distractions that take a leader away from the task at hand. One suggestion to avoid becoming bogged down by interruptions is to give a quick yes or no answer to a question, but put off longer discussions since they require "your individual attention" which is at the time being given to other priority work. Schedule a convenient time later on for detailed discussion.

Some work environments are more conducive to interruptions than others. The "open office" concept requires a determined effort to concentrate on the task at hand. Hang a sign that reads "my door is closed"—even if there isn't a door (remember Les Nessman from the TV sitcom *WKRP in Cincinnati*, who used yellow tape to mark off his office parameters)—when you are working on a project that requires your undivided attention.

Use voice mail and e-mail to save time. Use the telephone as a quick alternative to meetings whenever possible. Keep all the information you need at your fingertips before dialing, so there won't be the need to call back to clarify or gather missed data.

> "A man who chases two rabbits catches neither."
> CONFUCIUS

(ii) Procrastination

When the project, or the situation, looms difficult or unpleasant, we try to delay. My wife swears by her solution for procrastination. She breaks the job into small pieces, which she tackles one by one—and gives herself small rewards for completing each part of the task.

Psychologists say procrastination is a habit. Each time we do it, we reinforce its repetition. Force yourself to go ahead by beginning when your momentum is at a high, by telling someone about the job you are doing, by chipping away at it bit by bit, by making "doing it" a habit.

> **"Take time to deliberate; but when the time for action arrives, stop thinking and go in."**
>
> ANDREW JACKSON, (1767-1845)
> SEVENTH PRESIDENT OF THE UNITED STATES

(iii) Perfectionism

We all want to do well but perfectionists want to be perfect—placing demands on themselves and on those who work for them that are so high it is almost impossible for them to be successfully met. This often causes more time than is warranted to be spent on a project—making for a poor return on invested time. If you find you tend to have impossibly high expectations of yourself and others, ask yourself this question: what would be the impact on your organization, on your staff, on yourself, if you settled for just less than perfection? When you discover that the impact is not significant, convince yourself to lower your expectations and settle for a job well done. In today's busy work environment it doesn't make sense to waste time on being unnecessarily perfect.

> **"I'd much prefer an 'OK plan' executed with uncommon vigor right now, to the 'perfect plan,' executed in a humdrum fashion next week."**
>
> GENERAL GEORGE PATTON, (1885-1945)

(iv) Not Utilizing Available Resources

Either because they don't realize what resources are available, or because they are determined to do a job all by themselves, many leaders find they do not use available support to save themselves time. Such resources include staff, peers, technology, information and past experiences. By utilizing support or research staff, Internet technology, and past experiences to their utmost, your own time is managed more efficiently.

(v) Difficulty in Saying "No"

We're made to feel guilty when we refuse. It becomes much easier just to say "yes"—but not for long. Saying "yes" often leads to crisis, stress, fatigue and anger as we attempt to do more than is possible. Keep in mind you can't be everywhere—or everything—to everyone.

Practice saying "no." Practice until you are able to say "no" gently, but firmly; with empathy and understanding, yet resolutely. It will give you more than time. It will give you a sense of control and freedom—and it makes it easier to work for you.

Steve Kahn's challenge was to minimize everyday time-wasters. When he was CEO of Integrity QA Software, he couldn't find enough days in the week to do everything. He didn't have much of a support staff—an office manager and a very part-time CFO—so he felt he had to be very strict about how he allocated his time. His tips:

> **"'No' is an acceptable answer for many situations."**
>
> TOM MCNOWN, MANAGER, TRAINING & MARKETING
> GENERAL MOTORS OF CANADA LIMITED

- ◆ Set limits on people who take too much of your time. If a person takes too long to explain Kahn tells them, "Give me the short version." Or, "I've another ten minutes on this, so let's make sure we get the important stuff done." Then he smiles to avoid being perceived as rude.

- ◆ If a meeting is not a top priority, stay for the beginning then hand off to an associate.

- ◆ If you don't have time for something, just say so.

Janet Ryan's challenge is to find an alternative to compulsive scheduling. Partner of Ryan•Whiteman, she was completely controlled by "To Do" lists. She'd get to the end of the day and feel like she hadn't accomplished anything important. She re-evaluated how she was spending her time, and realized that she needed to be less structured. Her tips:

◆ Keep your schedule loose enough to allow for spontaneity.

◆ Don't be afraid to step back and ask if you've really accomplished anything.

◆ Give yourself permission for interruptions if you feel they are justified—they may be more important than anything you're scheduled to accomplish.

Everyone has their own way to manage time. Ask your staff, your peers and your friends how they save time. Adapt the ideas that interest you, that suit you and your environment, so you'll work smarter, not harder.

LEADERS' TIPS ON SAVING TIME

◆ "I eat a light lunch, so I don't get groggy in the afternoon."

◆ "I carry a small note pad to jot down notes and ideas."

◆ "I always plan at the end of the day for the next day—and set priorities."

◆ "I do first things first."

◆ "I always use Pareto's 80/20 principle."

◆ "I concentrate on one thing at a time."

◆ "I set deadlines for myself and others—and keep them."

◆ "I delegate as much as I possibly can."

◆ "I make use of experts to advise with special assignments, problems."

◆ "I put post-it™ notes up in my office to remind me of my goals."

◆ "I try to complete a project before taking a break."

DELEGATING

Today's leaders don't expect to solve all their organization's problems them-selves. They realize that sharing both the major and minor dilemmas to be faced—*and solved* with their staff makes good sense. So they delegate. It's one of the most valuable business tools of today's leaders—if used well. If delega-tion is used poorly, it's executive suicide. Delegating can offer a trio of signif-icant advantages to the leader: more time, an increased reach of the compa-ny's activity, effective development of staff.

It does not, however, come easily since you remain accountable for what you have delegated. This being the case, it is essential that you supervise the project to some extent. Involved, hands-on, mentor-style super-vision is recommended so you remain on top of the project, protecting your own accountability.

> "Delegating work works, provided the one delegating works, too."
>
> ROBERT HALF
> ROBERT HALF INTERNATIONAL INC.

The objective is to create a situation where those to whom the work has been delegated become in effect, extensions of yourself. They do the actual work with the same commitment, but not necessarily the same style or process, as you would have exhibited yourself. Recognizing the risks of delegating, it behooves an astute leader to be careful about what is delegated, how it is delegated and to whom it is delegated.

> "You can delegate authority, but you can never delegate responsibility by delegating a task to someone else. If you picked the right man, fine, but if you picked the wrong man, the responsibility is yours—not his."
>
> RICHARD E. KRAFVE, PRESIDENT
> RAYTHEON

Keep the ultimate goals of delegating in mind. They'll assist you to answer the questions posed on the next page.

BEFORE DELEGATING ASK:

◆ Is this project important enough to be delegated or
  should it be eliminated?

◆ Is it an effective use of time for those involved in the project?

◆ Have I explained the parameters of the project carefully?

◆ Does the person in charge have experience in this area?
  What resources can I supply to assist them?

◆ Have I explained how I wish to be appraised with the progress
  of the project? Daily meetings? Weekly reports?

◆ Have I the time to supervise effectively? What is my supervisory plan?

◆ How will the delegation of this project expand the capabilities
  of those involved?

Effective leaders realize they are unable to do the impossible, handle everything in their organization alone. They must be confident enough in themselves and their vision to park their egos at the door and delegate responsibility for the process and the planning so that their organizations move forward.

When leaders and their staff are not in sync, delegating effectively is impossible to do, as this story, relayed to me by one of my clients, indicates.

Bob Lessor's pride in being the top man made it hard for him to share authority. He tried, but he found to his dismay that his delegating capability was not as good as he thought. On his return from a short business trip, Lessor found a sheaf of payroll sheets. Snatching them up he stormed out of his office and shouted "Who approved all this overtime while I was away?"

"I did," the production chief answered. Realizing that all heads were turned to see what the shouting was about, Lessor lowered his voice.

Taking the production manager with him, Lessor stepped into his office. There he told the production man, "You've got your nerve authorizing overtime. This is still my company, and I'll decide what extra costs we'll take on. You know that our prices are not based on paying overtime rates."

"Right," the production man replied. "But you told me I was in full charge of production. You said I should keep pushing so I wouldn't fall behind on deliveries."

> "An outstanding leader must be able to suppress his ego and recognize that he does not have a cornerstone on brains."
>
> ARTHUR I. MOLL, PRESIDENT
> COMPAUDIT SERVICES

"That's right," Lessor said. "I remember writing you about a couple of orders just before I went out of town."

"Yes you did. And one of them—the big order—was getting behind, so I approved overtime."

"I guess I would have done the same thing if I had been here," Lessor said. "But let's get things straight for the future. From now on, overtime needs my okay. We've got to keep costs in line."

Had he clarified the authority that department heads had up front, Mr. Lessor would have saved himself a lot of time and effort.

Delegating effectively requires pre-planning as one of my workshop participants, explained. Hank Ebbers told the group that competent people want to know exactly what they are being held responsible for. He described how he organized his small company into three departments: production , sales and an administrative department. The manager who handled production was responsible for advertising, customer solicitations and

> "Leaders must have low ego needs, because their main role is to let other people excel."
>
> KENNETH H. BLANCHARD, CHAIRMAN
> BLANCHARD TRAINING AND DEVELOPMENT INC.

customer service.

Hank regarded the administrative department as the headquarters and the service unit for the other two departments. Its manager was responsible for personnel, purchasing and accounting. Hank also worked out with his assistants the practices and procedures necessary to get the job done. His assistants were especially helpful in pointing out any overlaps or gaps in assigned responsibilities. He then put all the procedures into writing.

Each supervisor had a detailed statement of the function of each department and the extent of each department's authority. This statement included a list of specific actions which they could take on their own and a list of actions which required approval from Hank or, in his absence, the assistant general manager.

Hank had thought about the times he might be absent from the plant. To make sure that things would keep moving, the production manager was designated as the assistant general manager and was given authority to make all operational decisions in Hank's absence.

In thinking about absences, Hank went one step further. He instructed each department head to designate and train an assistant who could run their department if the need arose.

By outlining the chain of delegation as well as the reasons for choosing the process he did, Hank was able to get his staff onside. Once the procedure was instituted he enabled staff to execute the power he had given them.

He also looked beyond his company's immediate needs to what requirements there might be in six months or in a year's time and encorporated the flexibility needed to deal with that eventuality whenever it would occur. He emphasized that when you spell out delegation in detail much less is left to happenstance.

TIPS FOR SUCCESSFUL DELEGATIING

◆ Determine how and to whom to distribute the physical work, so staff do not become stressed out and ineffective.

◆ Be willing to delegate jobs you would rather do yourself, but don't really have the time to do, to those who would probably do as well or better than you.

◆ Delegate, don't abdicate.

◆ Stay informed but don't stifle others' enthusiasm and energy.

◆ Don't dictate the method to be used—only clarify the goals. Very often staff will come up with a better method than yours.

◆ Check progress of the project at each stage, so that corrective action can be taken should something go awry.

◆ Take the time to delegate to weaker members of the team, so they will have the opportunity to grow and develop.

◆ Use delegating to develop the skills, talents and capabilities of those involved.

◆ Demonstrate your trust. Delegate not only responsibility for the project, but authority to accomplish it. Final accountability, however, always rests with you.

RESOLVING CONFLICT

Conflict is a normal part of both our personal and business lives since we all maintain various, and often opposing, goals. Conflict does not have to be adversarial if the conflict is managed rather than allowed to escalate into an out-of-control situation.

"Whether one is negotiating with customers, vendors, employees, members of family, leaders know and understand the importance of building consensus."

BERNIE BRILL, EXECUTIVE VICE PRESIDENT SMART

As a positive force it can keep our lives stimulating, creative, innovative, and action-filled. As an impetus to confront issues, to stimulate change and to encourage positive resolution, conflict can be beneficial.

However when conflict destroys morale, divides groups and affects productivity, it is harmful and must be resolved.

CONTROLLED CONFLICT:

◆ strengthens relationships and supports teamwork;

◆ encourages open communication and cooperative problem solving;

◆ resolves disagreements quickly, thereby increasing productivity;

◆ deals with the issues and works toward a win/win resolution;

◆ makes allies and diffuses anger;

◆ brings out into the open all sides of an issue in a positive, supportive environment;

◆ de-stresses and focuses attention toward results.

UNCONTROLLED CONFLICT:

◆ damages relationships and discourages cooperation;

◆ harbors defensiveness and hidden agendas;

◆ wastes time, money and human resources;

◆ focuses on fault-finding and blaming;

◆ creates hard feelings and enemies;

◆ is frustrating, stress producing and energy draining;

◆ is disruptive, hostile and becomes part of the problem, rather than part of the solution.

As a leader, it would be wonderful to prevent destructive conflict altogether. But business being what it is, conflict cannot be completely eliminated. The best strategy to minimize or counteract conflict is through effective management. Skillful planning, organizing, directing, leading, coordinating and facilitating of your people is essential.

To avoid destructive conflict Harley-Davidson Inc. involves their people from top to bottom. The Harley Leadership Institute focuses on three competencies Harley-Davidson believes all employees should have: communication skills, conflict resolution ability and team skills. On the outside the Harley image may be tough, but the company is growing based on the "soft skills" employees demonstrate.

To constructively and effectively manage conflict resolution there are some basic skills, and guidelines to consider:

GUIDELINES FOR CONSTRUCTIVE CONFLICT RESOLUTION

1. Some conflicts may be better left unresolved

2. Personality and attitude affect the outcome of a conflict or disagreement. Attack the problem, not the person. Criticize the activity or procedure, but be prepared to offer practical solutions for improving it. The flip side of the privilege of criticizing is the responsibility for improving.

3. Know when to give feedback—when to watch—when to listen.

   Search for a win/win solution. There are only real winners when both sides are satisfied.

4. Communicate without attributing blame. Use an "I" message. "I'm feeling…."

   Disagree firmly but with tact using your own feelings to explain, rather than attributing blame by focusing on what someone else did. As an example you could say "I'm feeling concerned that the quarterly report won't be completed in time to share with the board" rather than "you'd better hurry up and finish the report so it will be completed in time to share with the board."

5. Often there are underlying areas of contention beyond what is on the surface, that are the real conflict culprits. Understand and deal honestly with the real issues behind the conflict.

6. Be responsible for your emotions. No one makes you angry—you become angry yourself. Understand and take charge of your feelings and behaviors, but don't allow them to effect "the work."

7. Express yourself clearly and concisely, without anger, sarcasm or accusation.

   Look forward toward solutions and new opportunities, not backward toward blaming and recriminations.

8. Use cooperation and accurate communication to succeed.
   Search out and identify areas where there are similar perspectives,
   where collaboration can take place. The leader can serve as a mediator
   or facilitator to settle disputes with the parties involved, if necessary.
   As a last resort the leader will resolve disputes.

9. Find and communicate a goal that transcends the biased, narrow
   objectives of either person or group.

10. Use a mix n' match strategy to retard provincialism and encourage
    cross-fertilization of ideas and strategies among staff. Moving staff to
    different groups creates a revitalized environment. New combinations
    of staff share different perspectives on a situation, come up with
    different solutions and breathe new vigor into their environment.

Vilfredo Pareto, the Italian economist who gave us the 80/20
principle (80% of our sales come from 20% of our merchandise), also gave us
the "Pareto Efficient" concept. This refers to an efficient resolution of conflict
in which no other agreement besides the one arrived at would result in *both*
parties being any better off. The Pareto Efficient concept provides an
excellent win/win perspective from which to view conflict resolution.
Consider this simple example and apply it to your quest for gaining an
efficient agreement to your negotiations.

Barry and Nancy are going out to dinner. Barry likes Indian food best
and cannot eat Chinese food. Nancy greatly prefers Chinese food but finds
Indian dishes too hot. What would serve as the best solution for both? They
could go to a Chinese or Indian restaurant, but this would result in either
Barry or Nancy being dissatisfied; they could choose another option. They
both like Italian but prefer Thai food to Italian.

It is possible to plot out all these choices on a graph. On one axis are Barry's preference values. On the other axis are the values Nancy attaches to each preference. For Barry Indian food has the highest value. Thai is next, then Italian and Chinese is last. For Nancy, Chinese is highest, followed by Thai, Italian and Indian is the last.

Since both Barry and Nancy prefer Thai to Italian, a decision to go to a Thai restaurant results in both Barry and Nancy being better off than if they had gone to an Italian restaurant. The Thai choice is Pareto efficient because the only choice that is better for Barry (Indian) leaves Nancy worse off. Similarly, the only decision better for Nancy (Chinese) leaves Barry worse off.

MAKING DECISIONS

Chris Davis of Sears Home Central states that "the willingness to make tough and timely decisions, and deal with the resulting naysayers and pessimists with stoic professionalism and understanding is the mark of a leader." Unfortunately this skill does not come with "how-to" instructions. As a result many leaders are inclined to make quick decisions (to get it over with), slow decisions (in the effort to avoid error), or procrastinate for so long that in the end there is no decision to make—it has already been made.

> "It often happens that I wake up at night and begin to think about a serious problem and decide I must tell the Pope about it. Then I wake up completely and remember that I am the Pope."
>
> POPE JOHN XXIII

> "A leader is a man who makes decisions. Sometimes they turn out right and sometimes they turn out wrong; but either way, he makes them."
>
> MUTUAL BENEFIT LIFE INSURANCE CO.

Studies repeatedly show that the most productive leaders are excellent decision makers. They take charge of the situation, deciding the future of their organization, rather than being buffeted by the winds of indecision or procrastination.

Doug Raymond, President and CEO of the Retail Advertising and Marketing Association adds that a strong leader needs to possess the ability "to follow their own instincts. Information overload is a reality. Sometimes the gut is the only visible counsel they'll have or need. Most importantly, a strong leader needs the courage to make the right choices. We are entering a new era, an era which the only successful companies will be those who establish a trusting relationship with their customers, who demonstrate a commitment to their communities, who recognize an obligation to the common good that far exceeds shareholder concerns. To make the right choices, to set a mission that encompasses responsibility in a truly visionary way, and to stay the course, will take courage. Strong leaders will demonstrate that courage, the others will go away."

> **"People within an organization or allied to an organization expect leaders to be able to make tough decisions; delaying a tough decision or not making it can be viewed as being weak."**
>
> TOM MCNOWN, MANAGER, TRAINING & MARKETING
> GENERAL MOTORS OF CANADA LIMITED

BECOME A BETTER DECISION MAKER BY ASKING AND ANSWERING THESE EIGHT QUESTIONS:

1. What is the real decision that must be made?

Determining the real problem controls the process. Look at the problem from various points of view to ensure that the decision you are making actually addresses the issue. For example, the report on profit is not what was expected. Assuming that profits would increase by laying off staff, the decision becomes who and when. But ask yourself if this course of action will really solve the problem, or would making a different decision provide a more effective means to solve the problem at hand?

2. What is your goal in making the decision?

This will direct your decision making. Consider both short-term and longer-term goals. In the example just cited, from a short-term perspective you want to increase profitability. From a longer-term perspective you might want to grow your company and expand your area of expertise.

3. What experience(s) can you remember to assist you to make the decision?

Think back. Looking backward effectively involves searching for patterns in various experiences and creating links that were perhaps not apparent previously. It requires analyzing different cause-and-effect situations to determine whether they shed new light on your current situation. In our example, you might recall that in the past, each time profits were down, blame was established and some staff were fired. You might also recall that your competitor, now a global giant, reduced the salary of management, but held onto staff during tough times. While ruminating through previous experiences, business strategy experts advise, be aware and wary of protecting old decisions—it is not necessary to defend them any longer.

4. Who can assist you to make the decision?

Determine who has had appropriate experiences and who is currently involved in the problem or in a similar problem. If, as in our example, the situation involves frontline staff, it might be helpful to get input from people who are involved in day-to-day operations and from other leaders who are encountering similar decision making challenges.

5. What options do you, and those whose counsel you seek, see as possible?

If there aren't any alternatives, there is no need to make a decision—however, check that all possible options have been explored. Your decision can only be as good as your most informed option.

6. What would be the probable outcome of each decision?

Again take both a short-term and a long-term perspective. Use your rearview mirror and gaze into your crystal ball. Come up with an appropriate list of consequences for each decision.

> "An effective leader must have the ability to make a decision and stick with that decision."
>
> KIM STRUBLE, CMP, DIRECTOR, MEETINGS & EXPOSITIONS
> AMERICAN LOGISTICS ASSOCIATION

7. What are the pros and cons?

Consider the benefits and the risks. Sometimes it's easiest to list all the positive consequences on one side of a sheet of paper and the negative consequences on the other. Another helpful technique is to give each consequence a numerical value based on its importance.

8. When is it time to make a decision?

Once everything has been considered, go for it. Don't permit yourself to get trapped in indecision. Indecision or decision paralysis—even after all the consideration, assistance and analysis is done—is not uncommon, but it is crippling to a leader. You can always fix a bad decision, but you can't fix indecision.

Thinking back, the most memorable case of good decision making, exercised courageously, that I can remember was during the Tylenol crisis.

In 1984 it was discovered that Tylenol bottles on store shelves had been tampered with, leaving the contents seriously compromised. Seven deaths were reported. Johnson & Johnson immediately recalled Tylenol bottles on a national level—31 million bottles of extra-strength Tylenol capsules were removed from merchants' shelves. This was a far-reaching decision—made with speed and certainty to prevent any further poisoning.

"Deliberate with caution, but act with decision, and yield with graciousness, or oppose with firmness."

CHARLES CALEB COLTON, (1780-1832)
ENGLISH CLERIC, SPORTSMAN AND WINE MERCHANT

Tylenol soon reappeared on store shelves in tamper proof bottles—a safety feature quickly copied by other manufacturers. Chairman of the Board at the time, James E. Burke's excellent judgment turned a potentially disastrous situation for Tylenol into a triumph of leadership, of brand loyalty and customer trust.

Think outside the box. "Invent" different approaches to become better. Ensure that your decision making demonstrates to the marketplace the advantages and benefits of your organization, of your staff. Make your organization memorable.

Management gurus and strategists alike agree that it is better to have made a decision poorly than not to have made one at all. We all learn from our mistakes; but if we do nothing we don't accomplish anything or learn anything. Keep in mind that doing nothing is making a choice.

"If you take risks, you may still fail. But if you do not take risks, you will surely fail. The greatest risk of all is to do nothing."

ROBERTO GOIZUETA, FORMER CHAIRMAN & CEO
THE COCA-COLA COMPANY

STAMP OUT INDECISION

1. Delay making a decision until you have enough information, but no longer. Waiting until every piece of the puzzle is in place makes the decision a foregone conclusion.

2. Get ideas, suggestions and assistance from others, but be careful in soliciting involvement from too many people. It slows down the process considerably.

3. Delegate the decision to those directly involved in the situation on a daily basis. Often decisions are made more effectively by those close to the circumstances.

4. Brainstorm. Holding an invigorating session with key people could easily produce ideas not previously considered, or expand alternatives to ideas already put forward.

5. Allocate decision making time related to the importance of the decision. If the outcome of the decision making is inconsequential don't waste too much time with it.

6. Revisit frustrating decisions. Leave a difficult decision for a few hours or even longer, while you do other work. If you can afford another day, sleep on it. It worked for Einstein. Come back to the decision later, with renewed vigor.

Would you work for you?   Yes ☐   No ☐   I'm not sure at this time ☐

SOME TOUGH QUESTIONS

1. Think through your hiring process. Where do its strengths lie? Where do its weaknesses lie? What can be done to improve the process?

_____

_____

_____

_____

2. What do you see as the advantages of hiring online? Disadvantages? What elements of online hiring could you use effectively?

_____

_____

_____

_____

3. Think through your interview process. What changes have you made to the process in the last five years? How effective are your interviewing skills? What could you do to improve them?

_____

_____

_____

_____

4. What advantages have you found in using the team approach?
   What disadvantages? What can be changed in your teams
   to turn disadvantages into advantages?

_____

_____

_____

_____

5. What feedback, assistance or information have you culled from team members
   to improve the team?

_____

_____

_____

_____

_____

6. Is effective time management one of your strengths or one of your weaknesses?
   How can you share your effective time management strategies? How can you
   improve your weak time management strategies?

_____

_____

_____

_____

_____

7. How do you minimize interruptions? How do you eliminate procrastination? How do you say "no" effectively? What else could you do to minimize interruptions, eliminate procrastination and say "no" effectively?

_____

_____

_____

_____

8. How effective is your delegating strategy? What makes it not as effective as you would like? What strategies can you incorporate to make it more effective?

_____

_____

_____

_____

9. How do you rate your conflict resolution skills? Why? What techniques could improve your conflict resolution skills?

_____

_____

_____

_____

10. Recognizing your skills, would you work for you?

_____

_____

_____

CHAPTER 5

MAKING CONNECTIONS

Would You Work for You?
Yes, if Only... **You Know How to Communicate Effectively**

All the skills leaders require to ensure that their people are happy to work for them are important to acquire and to practice, however, effective communication is absolutely essential. If asked whether we are effective communicators, the vast majority of us would reply, *"yes! we communicate well."* We all assume we are clear, concise and accurate communicators. We think that we speak well, are clearly understood and are effective listeners.

We aren't!

For the kind of leaders you would work for, effective communication is not an option. Knowing how to communicate but not doing it doesn't count.

> "If you can't listen and learn, if you can't explain and tell, you ain't going nowhere."
>
> DENNIS WATSON, VICE PRESIDENT & GENERAL MANAGER
> CKCO TELEVISION

Communication is more than just transmitting or receiving information accurately. It is making connections. It is developing a network through which the hard facts and the emotional ownership of information flow to all participants. Quite a challenge! Why is it in this hi-tech Information Age, our biggest problems are so integrally tied to sending and receiving accurate information?

Leaders have tremendous responsibility to communicate accurately since doing so impacts their people so dramatically. Based on the perceived communication, staff decides how to allocate *their* time and energies. Before every interaction, ask yourself a series of questions. What do I want to convey—exactly? What is *my* motivation for saying what I do? How do I want my people to act as a result of what I've said? How do I double check that what I've said has been perceived accurately? How do I double check that what I've heard is what has been told to me? Leaders who can answer these questions satisfactorily have a much better chance at successful communication.

> "Care should be taken, not that the reader may understand, but that he must understand."
>
> QUINTILIAN, (35–95)
> ROMAN RHETORIC TEACHER

Consider each of these areas of communication, and you'll realize the enormity of the challenge—and the extent of the opportunity.

WRITING

The written word communicates loudly and clearly, often more loudly and more clearly than we realize. The memos and e-mails, not to mention formal letters, we shoot off daily speak volumes about us. From the words we choose, to our grammar and spelling, to the sign-off, we are evaluated and judged—and sometimes hired—based on our writing ability.

> "Advocates [of electronic mail] love to push the benefits of direct communication. Managers send and receive messages on a one-to-one basis. Now that secretaries don't fix their sloppy writing, the whole world wonders how they passed English 1A."
>
> DAVID J. BUERGER, PROFESSOR
> SANTA CLARA UNIVERSITY

Not long ago I had a discussion about e-mail with my son, a Professor of Law, and several of his friends. The conversation centered on the acceptable format of e-mail. The general feeling at the start seemed to be that e-mail afforded an opportunity for brief, unstructured communication—sent off, without a second glance, by the click of a button. But is it? As the conversation continued, however, it became apparent that we judge, and are indeed judged, not only by the vocabulary chosen to communicate the message, but also by its spelling and grammar.

My son declared that after considerable contemplation he has decided to sign all his e-mails M.G.—not too formal, as Professor M. Geist would be, yet not too familiar. He considered the perception of the reader in his decision. The written word reinforces the image we hold of others and they hold of us. By the end of our talk, it became apparent that simple e-mail—*isn't*. It is one more form of written communication that offers great benefits or significant challenges to every leader depending upon when the "send" button is pressed.

> "The writer does the most who gives his reader the most knowledge, and takes from him the least time."
>
> CHARLES CALEB COLTON, (1780-1832)
> ENGLISH CLERIC

Communication experts I spoke with offered the following five tips to remove obstacles from written communications, regardless whether the writing was electronic or by hand.

1. Write concisely, using vocabulary that is understood by all who are to read it. Reread from the recipient's viewpoint, to ensure that information will not be misconstrued. Distribute in an efficient manner, so the recipient receives your message in sufficient time to take appropriate action.

2. Make communication easy to read. Clear type, sized and spaced for speed and efficiency is essential.

3. Include graphs, charts and visuals to assist in clarifying more complicated concepts. Visuals also aid in increasing the information retained more accurately.

4. Use a consistent format as a precursor to content. For example newsletters formatted in a consistent manner are expected to include similar information from one issue to the next, and will be read with this in mind. Interested in presenting "New!" "Exciting!" "Ground Breaking" information? Use a different format that conveys the unique feeling of this information.

5. Consider the timing of written communication. Information sent on a Friday at 4 pm, will not receive the same attention as information sent on Monday at 10:30 am. This applies equally to information disseminated at holiday time, just before vacations or immediately after a huge project has been dumped on a team.

> "This report, by its very length, defends itself against the risk of being read."
>
> WINSTON CHURCHILL, (1874-1965)
> BRITISH PRIME MINISTER, AUTHOR, SOLDIER

SPEAKING

When we speak we are eager to share our ideas, thoughts and feelings with others. We feel we have so much to contribute that we often go on and on, just to ensure that our information has been received. Experts in communication emphasize, however, that rarely can you inform, enlighten, motivate, stimulate and get feedback all in a single message. They advise taking a narrowly focused approach rather than taking a broad sweeping one. Simplify! Stay on target in order to communicate what is of primary importance. Ensure that whatever you are

> "But words once spoke can never be recalled."
>
> HORACE, (65-8 BC)
> ROMAN POET

> "Complexity alienates whereas simplicity invites."
>
> ANONYMOUS

communicating is actually being received—accurately. This is often easier said than done. Accurate communication requires that signs of defensiveness, or lack of trust or absence of confidence be eliminated from the transmission. These negative signals send up a red flag, promptly causing listeners to reject the message completely. Accurate communication also requires that listeners feel they are being talked to on an equal footing with the speaker. "Talking down" to them is guaranteed to produce a negative response.

The chance for accurate communication increases when interference is minimized. Eliminate "white noise" with these additional suggestions.

> "Communicate unto the other guy that which you would want him to communicate unto you if your positions were reversed."
>
> AARON GOLDMAN, CEO
> THE MACKE COMPANY

- ◆ Accept the responsibility to share your ideas, information and feelings by ensuring the environment is conducive to transmitting these ideas, information and feelings to the listener. Make certain the surroundings are comfortable — well lit, appropriate temperature, clean. Make certain outside distractions are eliminated. The optimum listening conditions can only enhance the listening experience.

- ◆ Don't be stingy with information. Drowning the listener in extraneous details is counterproductive, but at the same time providing sufficient information so that the listener feels like a participant rather than an observer is most beneficial.

- ◆ Always keep the listener's perspective at the forefront of your thoughts. As my son, Josh, has reminded me on several occasions, "it doesn't much matter what you intend for me to receive from your comments — it only matters what I feel I received." Listeners have three vital questions they want answered in any discourse. What's in it for me? How will it affect me? What course of action is afforded me? Answer them before you begin.

> "Whatever people think, is."
> OTIS SINGLETARY, CHANCELLOR
> UNIVERSITY OF KENTUCKY

◆ Be clear, organized, brief and to the point. Look for signs of comprehension from your listener, such as slight nods, smiles or eye contact. When you see frowning, or a furrowed brow, rapid eye movements, check to ensure that your listener has understood you.

◆ Know the listener. What turns them on—what turns them off—what makes them tune out completely. Press the buttons that will elicit the response you are seeking.

◆ In addition to considering the listener, consider the situation and the objective before you begin. This may alter how, when or in what context your intended remarks are made.

◆ Be sensitive to how you are being perceived. Recognize the quality of the existing relationship, that is the level of trust and respect between you and your listener. Without trust and respect, little is believed or accepted.

◆ Be aware of inadvertent conclusions that the listener may read into the message.

◆ Rehearse the message, matching speed of delivery to the listener's capacity for comprehension.

◆ Ask questions of the listener to confirm that the message has been received and understood.

THE VALUE OF BEING ASSERTIVE

One matter that needs to be addressed at this point in the discussion about communication is the fine line between assuring that demands are met and being too compliant. The principles of assertiveness, which noted psychologists have incorporated into behavioral therapy for many years, have also found their way to the forefront of business management development. Today, it is essential for all leaders to be assertive—that is, to be able to express their thoughts, feelings and beliefs in direct, honest and appropriate ways without abusing the rights and privileges of others. Especially in difficult situations such as poor performance reviews, disciplining and firing, assertiveness can be very useful. In less adversarial circumstances, adopting an assertive stance facilitates providing praise and positive reinforcement.

> **"The worse the news, the more effort should go into communicating it."**
>
> ANDY GROVE, CEO
> INTEL CORP.

Assertiveness is usually associated with both "the right to do something" and "the responsibility for doing something." For example you have the right to express your anger, but you are also responsible for expressing it in a socially acceptable manner. Assertive behavior incorporates in its tenets the concern for one's own rights as well as the rights of others, whereas passive behavior negates the importance of our own rights, and aggressive behavior negates the importance of others' rights.

In its non-verbal form assertiveness includes good eye contact, relaxed posture and a well-modulated speaking voice. Verbally assertive communication incorporates "I" statements such as, "I feel concerned when I see customers' needs not being met" and cooperative expressions of a situation such as, "we have a problem"—rather than "you have a problem."

Assertive communication is not a panacea for all ills within an organization. It does, however, offer an astute leader an excellent set of skills because it helps to ensure a win/win outcome in both positive and potentially negative situations, ensuring that everyone in the organization feel they are on an equal foot.

After each session that I conduct, participants come up and ask how I manage to be so at ease speaking in front of a large group. They usually follow this up by saying that they could never do it.

I explain that I've been speaking for many years and the ease comes with practice. I go on to reassure them that they too would be able to speak effectively, if they follow the suggestions above.

LISTENING

"Listen. Don't explain or justify."
WILLIAM G. DYER, (1925-1997)
AUTHOR

It's a tough job, but someone's got to do it. Everyone wants to be listened to—unfortunately few of us have the self-discipline or the know-how to listen well ourselves.

We fail at listening for many reasons:

♦ We are primarily self-centered. We're interested in us, and what we have to say. We would rather speak than listen.

♦ We listen three to six times faster than anyone talks so we get bored, daydream and escape to our own little world.

♦ Our minds wander. We listen marginally. We're thinking about our retort, ready to make a verbal response.

♦ From experience we know there is little substance in all those words we hear and we lose interest. We listen to bits and assume we know it all.

♦ We get turned off by something in the speaker—attire, accent, repetition of certain words or mannerisms—and we tune out.

♦ We interrupt, most anxious to get our own word in.

The onus is on you to become an effective listener. Even if you consider yourself as skilled a listener as you would want to work for, you can become better by following these eight steps.

1. Admit that you can always become better. Be interested in improving your listening skills.

2. Recognize that speakers have at least two motivations for speaking: they feel they have something of value to say and they feel their comments are of importance to you.

3. Keep your eyes focused on the speaker while they're speaking, so that your mind doesn't wander.

4. Listen for the main points of what is being said. Hold on to them while you filter out the extraneous information. This is an effective method to combat boredom.

5. While listening, we often mentally prepare the points we want to make when it is our turn to speak. As we concentrate on our response, we lose the thread of what is being said. If possible find an association, such as an acronym, to remind you of the point you want to make and continue to listen. A possible alternative is to jot down a note.

6. Listen actively. Lean forward. Establish eye contact. Make appropriate gestures (head nod, intense posture, etc). Ask for clarification of comments. Paraphrase to ensure that you interpreted the remarks accurately. Be empathetic. Put yourself in the speaker's shoes—try to understand why they think the way they do.

7. Listen for what has not been said at all. Recognize instances where what has been verbalized does not really correspond with what has been implied.

8. Practice listening well. Everybody loves a good listener.

TEST YOUR LISTENABILITY

When you are listening do you...   YES   NO   SOMETIMES

1. Empty your mind of preconceived ideas,   ❑   ❑   ❑
   notions and biases?

2. Give your undivided attention to the speaker?   ❑   ❑   ❑

3. Listen from the speaker's perspective?   ❑   ❑   ❑

4. Listen for what has not been said?   ❑   ❑   ❑
   (it's sometimes very telling)

5. Listen without interrupting?   ❑   ❑   ❑

6. Give feedback by providing encouraging   ❑   ❑   ❑
   gestures, making appropriate comments and
   asking brief questions?

7. Listen in order to discuss, rather than argue   ❑   ❑   ❑
   or refute?

8. Listen to what is being communicated rather   ❑   ❑   ❑
   than concentrating on how it is being
   expressed?

9. Listen for both the intellectual and the   ❑   ❑   ❑
   emotional content?

10. Reiterate the speaker's point of view before   ❑   ❑   ❑
    you explain yours, especially if you disagree?

Leaders have been known to test and improve their listening skills using theatrics. The elements of the improv code—listening, accepting, initiating and contributing—enable effective business communication. These are the elements that are essential for today's leaders, says Joe Keefe,

Co-founder and Executive Producer of Second City Communications (a branch of The Second City Theatre). "Business people need to learn to open themselves up to a new idea fully, vulnerably, patiently and accurately. They must allow time to listen emotionally." Keefe feels that it is necessary to listen emotionally and physically, rather than react, in order to understand. The opportunity to participate in an improvisation-focused workshop assists leaders to listen in new and creative ways—a great boon for the speaker.

Listening is especially important to Chesterton Blumenauer Binswanger International Ltd., a global real estate conglomerate. Clive Mendelow, its Vice-chairman and Chief Operating Officer (COO) realizes that in order to hire and retain the type of staff they require—relationship - oriented, flexible, able to recognize the resources that must be marshaled to anticipate customer needs—Binswanger must be "listening very carefully to what [staff are] they're looking for... so that you've given them what they themselves want." In today's global marketplace the creation of international partnerships require astute listening skills.

Jim Tocher, CEO of NTS Computer Systems Ltd. said it so well, "God gave us two ears and one mouth. Use them in that proportion." Effective listening offers so many benefits and has no downside whatsoever. Prepare yourself to be a better listener and then assess your success afterwards.

UNDERSTANDING

In his book *Seven Habits of Highly Effective People,* Stephen Covey suggests a communication strategy that makes for more successful leaders—and happier, more contented followers. "Seek first to understand, then to be understood."

This clearly orients your communication focus toward understanding others *first.* It implies you are interested in who they are, where they come from,

"Franklin (Delano Roosevelt) had a good way of simplifying things. He made people feel he had a real understanding of things and they felt they had about the same understanding."

ELEANOR ROOSEVELT
AMERICAN STATESWOMAN AND HUMANITARIAN

what it is they are trying to communicate and why and what is really important to them. When you show interest in understanding, you demonstrate compassion and willingness to really listen and respond on an equal level—rather than exclusively focusing inward on your own wants, needs and interests. You will be amazed to discover that your eagerness to understand others is quickly mirrored by their interest and willingness to understand you.

Once a relationship based on reciprocal understanding has been established, the next step is to ensure that the listener accurately receives the intended information. Frequently this doesn't happen because we don't determine at the time whether our message has been understood—we just assume it has. An easy way to verify how much of your message has been received is simply to ask "would you please repeat the essence of what I've explained. I want to check myself to make sure I've communicated effectively."

When looking over work that has been submitted by a subordinate, or when checking out decisions that have been made as a result of a discussion, meeting or memo in which you were involved, do you ever find that the results bear little resemblance to your expectations? Could you have been so obtuse in your explanation, or was the listener not hearing or processing the information accurately?

We see evidence of this lack of understanding—this miscommunication—every day in today's business environments. We see information we were certain was understood misinterpreted, misfiled, misdirected or ignored. The challenge is to ensure that our communication is understood in the way we intended. We are also challenged to understand staff communication to us.

However, if a leader maintains a poor relationship with staff—either because they are anxious to be "one of the boys" or because they maintain a distant, aloof posture, staff may not communicate accurately to *them*—afraid to discuss the problem or taking the problem to an inappropriate person. Before any real communication can take place, the pipelines must be unclogged.

While not able to control every aspect of every communication encounter, you certainly are able to ensure that you understand the people with whom you communicate and that you control the dissemination of your own information. Additionally, it is incumbent upon you to make sure you've accurately understood what has been related to you. We are often certain we've understood, only to find later on that we haven't. The simplest way to avoid this trap is to repeat the gist of what has just been said and ask if your interpretation is accurate. This simple technique prevents misunderstandings later.

READING

Reading is also an aspect of the communication process, since you often act on what you've read, discuss what you've read and pass on or discard information you have read. Accurate interpretation of written information is therefore an important communication skill. Highlighters are an excellent tool for ensuring that the main ideas of a written piece are visually evident—easy to collect, review and remember. They'll assist you to retain valuable gems of information quickly.

"Reading maketh a full man; conference a ready man; and writing an exact man."

FRANCIS BACON, (1561-1624)
LORD CHANCELLOR OF ENGLAND

One of my wife's memories from university is of a girl sitting next to her in the lecture hall marking up her notes with three or four different colored highlighters. Each color represented a different type of information—enabling her to find and browse through specific data very quickly. This approach is certainly most applicable to our workplace today.

Hone your reading skills by summarizing, orally or in writing, what you've read. Test yourself by giving it to someone else and asking them to do a summary as well. Discuss the material to see if the material was interpreted the same way by both of you. If it wasn't, discuss the differences and determine why. Finally review the material again—shortly before it is to be presented or discussed. Review not only refreshes your thoughts, it often illuminates new ideas, that had gone unnoticed before.

My daughter-in-law, a family physician, reads her medical journals with a singular purpose: to keep herself abreast of the newest medical information, so she can provide the best, updated care for her patients. She always makes notes in the margins to personalize the information and then photocopies and files the articles in folders related to the subject. She reviews the material whenever she has a patient who comes in with problems similar to those described in the journal articles. She reads to stay on top of things because her patients' good health depends on it. Outstanding leaders read to stay on top of things because the good health of their organizations depend on it.

MEETINGS

To meet or not to meet that is the question. Meetings have always seemed to go part-and-parcel with business life. Well organized, well run meetings are a boon to effective communication. Haphazard, hastily thrown together meetings, on the other hand, are generally a waste of time. Since no one can afford that, it behooves anyone responsible for organizing meetings—store managers, section heads, floor supervisors or project directors— and everyone who is required to attend them to ensure that the meeting accomplishes what it's been designed to achieve: the communication of information, clearly, concisely and completely, so productive action can be taken.

THE MEETING RULES

1. Be flexible with timing. There is little point in holding the "Monday morning meeting" on Monday morning if there is nothing to discuss.

2. Schedule out-of-office meetings at the start or the end of the day. Breaking up the day to travel back and forth wastes time.

3. Schedule internal meetings with a built-in end, just before lunch or near the end of the day. No one will want the meeting to run late.

4. Control the size of the meeting. Only those necessary to make decisions should attend. The smaller and more controlled a meeting is, the quicker and more productive it will be.

5. Prepare and distribute an agenda prior to the meeting, with the most important items at the top:

    - *objective of meeting*   - *meeting start/end time*

    - *names of all attendees*   - *items to be discussed*

    - *presentations to be made/by whom*   - *length of time allocated to each item*

6. Afford participants sufficient preparation time.

7. Don't attempt to cover too much during a meeting. Hastily dealt with items come back to haunt and inevitably squander time later.

"The first meeting was held in the Garden of Eden. Eve called the meeting but hadn't distributed an agenda. Adam wasn't prepared to discuss the apple issue. The snake kept interrupting the meeting, playing Devil's advocate. Jumping to the easiest alternative, a hastily sprung plan was put into action. Today, we live with the ramifications of that first ineffective meeting."

GEORGE HUYLER

8. Check out meeting facilities. Use a check list to ensure supplies and equipment are available.

9. Circulate any required reading ahead of time.

10. Make the meeting as interesting and fast-paced as possible. Use visuals, and props.

11. Keep the meeting on track. Don't allow it to be derailed or interrupted.

12. Distribute minutes promptly. Keep them brief but include:
    -decisions reached
    - follow-up actions to be taken, by whom, by when

13. Evaluate each meeting. Repeat procedures that were successful and look for areas that require improvement.

14. Keep in mind that a meeting is an environment for people to gather as a group; as such it creates the opportunity to share information, expertise and knowledge. Allow it to do that.

15. As a meeting participant it is your responsibility to arrive on time, be prepared, make and keep notes.

While the rules rule, occasionally it might be beneficial to set them aside and energize staff with a different type of meeting. That's what Ken Talbot, CEO of Wizer, a business consultancy, does about once every two months. To encourage his staff to think "out of the box," to grow new ideas and to develop a broader perspective, he lets them play games. For the game "paper bag dramatics," he brings to the meeting an assortment of items such as an old photo, a toy truck, a scarf, a telephone, a computer disk and so on, in a paper bag. One person begins by taking one of the items out of the bag and starts to tell a story related to the item. Every couple of minutes the bag is passed to another person around the table who takes out another item and continues the story. Meeting participants get two minutes to take the story in a direction it has not yet gone. Everyone listens intently to make sure they can pick up the thread of the story. Everyone takes a risk and learns something both about themselves, and the rest of the group. As a result each member of the group begins to think a little differently and grows a little bit. The meeting becomes a brain stretcher—as all good meetings should be.

NON-VERBAL COMMUNICATION

Communication is much more than verbal. Gestures, body posture and facial expressions communicate quite strongly what we are thinking or feeling. In the 60s psychologists Paul Ekman and his associates laid the foundation for later studies that found that 70-90% of communication is non-verbal.

Being aware of non-verbal, in addition to verbal messages, affords tremendous advantages to every leader. Skill in interpreting non-verbal signals assists in garnering useful information about those with whom we communicate. An awareness of one's own non-verbal communication also assists in controlling what signals we send out to others.

Non-verbal communication includes:

- ◆ *body language*—facial expressions, body movements, gestures and posture;

- ◆ *physical space*—personal space, distance maintained in discussion;

- ◆ *personal attributes*—appearance, vocal cues, non-words (um, ahh, gasps, groans, etc.) and touch;

- ◆ *speech*—tone, speed, volume.

The messages that are sent via body language and personal attributes can be either conscious or subconscious, voluntary or involuntary. These non-verbal signals often communicate more emphatically, more powerfully than their verbal counterparts.

A hug, for example, is a conscious non-verbal expression of affection. Both giver and recipient are aware that the hug is a sign of friendship, warmth, affection. Well-dressed executives and people in uniform (police, military) convey success, respect and credibility, whereas carelessly attired or disheveled people show a lack thereof, to the subconscious mind of the recipient—unaware of the message they have received.

Eye contact, twitching and smiling indicate both voluntary and involuntary examples of either trust, open-mindedness, anxiety or untruthfulness depending on the specific signal given. Interpreting non-verbal communication, while not always easy, is of tremendous advantage—so much so that being aware of and consciously practicing this skill is recommended and taught by those who conduct leadership training sessions.

Whether communicating one-on-one, at meetings or on a negotiating team, be aware of the gestures and expressions that provide insight into your attitude and the attitudes of the people with whom you are communicating.

♦ Respect and honesty are demonstrated by eyes focused on those of the listener (no shifting, no avoiding eye contact).

♦ Confidence is often demonstrated by good body posture—head upright, back straight.

> "[General Eisenhower] and I didn't discuss politics or the campaign. Mostly we talked about painting and fishing. But what I remember most about the hour and a half I spent with him was the way he gave me all his attention. He was listening to me and talking to me, just as if he hadn't a care in the world, hadn't been through the trials of a political convention, wasn't on the brink of a presidential campaign."
>
> NORMAN ROCKWELL, (1894-1978)
> AMERICAN ARTIST

- Interest is demonstrated by the listener leaning slightly toward the speaker, sitting on edge of a chair, eyes focused on the speaker.

- Careful evaluation is demonstrated by a concentrating appearance, peering over eye glasses, cupping chin, little movement.

- Eagerness is often demonstrated by rubbing the hands together, smiling excessively, frequent nodding of the head.

- Deception or dishonesty is often demonstrated by frequent blinking, coughing, quick sideway glances or looking away while speaking.

- Defensiveness may be demonstrated by arms across chest, emphatic hand and arm gestures.

- Insecurity and anxiety is often demonstrated by constant fidgeting, nail-biting and hand-wringing.

- Frustration is often demonstrated by heavy breathing, rubbing of the neck, clenching fists.

- Boredom or indifference on the part of the listener may be demonstrated by glazed-over eyes, a preoccupied demeanor or aimless doodling.

Use your awareness and knowledge of body language to create a better, more effective communication environment to your advantage.

Several other interesting non-verbal communicators warrant mentioning. Meeting rooms and seating arrangements send out signals. Hence the establishment of King Arthur's Round Table where none of the participants was in a position of power of the table's "head." Consider the conditions of your meeting room. Dark, dingy, dirty rooms convey to the newcomer that the organization is slovenly—it conveys a lack of confidence.

Distance between participants is also a non-verbal issue. Keep in mind the need for personal space, realizing that different cultures have different requirements. Too much space indicates an emotional distance, not desirable for collaboration. Too little distance may be regarded as too intimate to be comfortable.

My sister-in-law, who works at a hospital, told me of a physician who after serving for several years in an African community, returned to her hometown. For the first few months of his return, he stood so close in conversation, he gradually backed whoever he was speaking with into the wall. Eventually he realized he was standing too close for comfort and stood at a more acceptable distance.

Vocal cues can also provide valuable information.
There are several speech attributes to consider:

- *volume*—too quiet impedes hearing, too loud sounds confrontational. Sometimes lowering your voice, is more effective than shouting.

- *pitch*—some changes are necessary to prevent boredom. A monotone loses the listener's attention. A high-pitched voice often indicates excitement, whereas a low pitched voice may indicate anger.

- *rate*—too slow is frustrating to listeners and often loses them. Too fast may indicate nervousness and may impede understanding. Attempt to mimic the rate of those with whom you are in discussion.

- *rhythm*—a regular rhythm conveys confidence and authority. Irregular rhythm may indicate uncertainty.

◆ *timing*—responding as soon as the last words leave the speaker's mouth may be interpreted as inappropriate—almost interrupting, too eager, not thought through. Response after a moment of silence may be interpreted as more thoughtful, more respectful.

◆ *articulation and pronunciation*—the degree of accuracy assists or impedes comprehension. Mispronunciation may be perceived as ignorance or incompetence.

Finally, the ubiquitous handshake communicates quite emphatically. A firm handshake, especially upon initial meeting, conveys power, confidence and sincerity. Loose handshakes convey wimpiness, insecurity. They are even considered insulting by some. A vice-like grip, aside from actually being painful, may send messages of intimidation or an overbearing demeanor in much of the world.

For mutually advantageous communication combine the firm handshake with a smile and direct eye contact. It conveys honesty and friendliness and puts people at ease. It really does set the stage for a positive, continuing relationship.

In order to build and maintain successful business relationships, every leader must communicate effectively, using both verbal and non-verbal messages, with sensitivity to the needs, interests, demands and viewpoint of others. It is a skill that can be mastered and demonstrated by all leaders who are willing to work toward enhancing their awareness and people skills—so that someone will want to work for them.

Would you work for you?   Yes ☐   No ☐   I'm not sure at this time ☐

SOME TOUGH QUESTIONS

1. Rate your writing skills on a scale of one to ten. What can you do tomorrow to improve your writing skills?

    _____

    _____

    _____

2. What organized plan can you develop to improve your writing skills for the long term?

    _____

    _____

    _____

3. Rate your speaking skills on a scale of one to ten. What can you do tomorrow to improve your speaking skills?

    _____

    _____

4. What resources can you use to improve your speaking skills for the long term?

    _____

    _____

5. What one change can you make in your communication efforts that will make you more assertive—but not aggressive?

    _____

    _____

6. Rate your listening skills on a scale of one to ten. What can you do tomorrow to improve your listening skills?

_____

_____

_____

7. What strategies can you develop to improve your listening skills for the long term?

_____

_____

_____

8. Do you "seek first to understand, then to be understood?" Give an example to explain.

_____

_____

_____

9. How do you ensure that you understand the information communicated to you? How do you ensure that others understand the information you communicate to them?

_____

_____

_____

10. Based on your communication skills, why would or wouldn't you work for you?

_____

_____

CHAPTER 6

MOVING FORWARD

Would You Work for You?
*Yes, if Only... **You Execute... Execute... Execute***

Once you are aware of all the elements that would encourage you to work for you, only one thing remains—*relentless consistent execution.* In a recent poll, top CEOs were asked for the motto they personally found most inspiring. A great many said their favorite was "Just do it!" Without perpetual execution the wheels simply grind to a halt.

"I find the great thing in this world is not so much where we stand, as in the direction we are moving. To reach the port of heaven, we must sail with the wind and sometimes against it—But we must sail, and not drift, nor lie at anchor."

OLIVER WENDELL HOLMES, (1809-1894)
AUTHOR

When I asked leaders what they felt was involved in effective execution of ideas, plan and policies and how they inspired their people they came up with these five prerequisites:

a) Maintain a clear vision.

b) Set goals.

c) Innovate.

d) Practice the ability to change.

e) Nurture a corporate culture.

MAINTAIN A CLEAR VISION

Today's leaders are expected to create a mighty vision for their companies of the possibilities, options and opportunities as yet undreamt of by others—and then share that vision so clearly that all who come in contact with it are inspired by it and magnetized to it for the long term. Modern leaders must be able to see paths where none previously existed and have the power to persuade others to follow them. They don't sit on the sidelines waiting for the future to happen, they direct the course it takes.

> "The most successful leader of all is one who sees another picture not yet actualized."
>
> MARY PARKER FOLLETT, (1863-1933)
> MANAGEMENT WRITER AND LECTURER

Visionaries are found in all walks of life, catalyzing the people around them. Jack Welch at General Electric, Bill Gates at Microsoft, Martin Luther King in the streets of Alabama, Winston Churchill at the cliffs of Dover, all held visions of the future, and what their roles were to make those visions come about. They were persistent in their vision, hardly realizing that their tenacity was exceptional rather than natural. This enabled them to see beyond the obstacles and move forward while everyone else was still rubbing their eyes—uncertain of what had just passed by.

Visionaries make their mark by breaking rules, taking risks and forging connections. They alter the landscape with innovations we are hardly aware we can not live without. They often create legends, make fortunes, inspire imitators and become household names. Great visionaries share the capacity to see what others don't or can't or won't and possess the courage to bring their visions to life.

> "Leaders are visionaries who have a sense of community, are focused on the future. Steadfast in their pursuit of goals."
>
> TERRY J. RUFFELL, PRESIDENT
> CANADIAN PROFESSIONAL SALES ASSOCIATION

Because "vision" is so personal, it is articulated slightly differently by each leader who defines it. Yet despite disagreement on the details, it is consistently embraced as a view of the future that requires change and support.

> **"Leadership is the capacity to translate vision into reality."**
>
> WARREN G. BENNIS, PRESIDENT
> UNIVERSITY OF SOUTHERN CALIFORNIA

Author Robert Fritz states that organizations, no matter their size, move forward in the wake of a clear, widely understood vision, since this state of affairs creates a tension between what exists and what could be. It pulls people to work together to close the gap. This unifying effect is especially valuable in organizations that consist of separate or distant departments. With the tremendous growth of virtual organizations, it is easy to realize the value of a consolidating vision. Organizations that have developed such an integrating vision are quick to recognize that their people all speak the same language, have common expectations of each other and operate from a common ground. Managers are delighted to add that when the vision reflects the needs and aspirations of a broad spectrum of the workforce, it improves performance significantly. It moves the organization forward.

> **"Change does not necessarily assure progress, but progress implacably requires change."**
>
> HENRY STEELE COMMAGER, (1902-1998)
> AUTHOR AND HISTORIAN

A visionary leader realizes that this warm and fuzzy sense of community is not an instant result of developing a vision. Growing a vision is an evolutionary process that requires continuous deliberation, action and re-evaluation. The many daily trials and experiences undertaken in this regard, afford everyone in the organization the opportunity to move closer to the perceived ideal.

> **"If you don't know where you're going, you will wind up somewhere else."**
>
> LAWRENCE PETER "YOGI" BERRA
> BASEBALL PLAYER AND COACH

Many organizational consultants advocate acting out a vision before launching it in writing. In the end however, both talk and action are necessary to realize an organizational vision. Too little discussion results in implementation that may not be coordinated or interpreted correctly, while too much discussion paralyzes efforts to actionize the vision.

The question is frequently raised, "does vision occur from the top-down or from the bottom-up?" Experts feel it is a bit of both. While it is generally agreed that the leader plays an instrumental role in conceiving and growing the vision, the actual author of the vision may be other than the leader. Research has shown that there are good reasons to involve staff at the start, since they will be the ones implementing the vision through the organizational rank and file. However, even if staff are not included at the very beginning, leaders must remember to discharge personal ownership of the vision to them when it is time for implementation, so staff will commit to the leader-directed vision as if it were their own.

> **"The shepherd always tries to persuade the sheep that their interests and his own are the same."**
>
> STENDHAL (MARIE HENRI BEYLE), (1783-1842)
> FRENCH NOVELIST AND BIOGRAPHER

President Dwight Eisenhower, when he was a general, used the push-pull theory to illustrate the responsibilities of a leader. He set a piece of string down on a table and pushed it with his fingers. Nothing more than a clump of twisted string resulted. However, when he pulled it, the line of string followed his finger as far as he wanted to take it.

Albert Schweitzer said it slightly differently, but no less effectively: *"Example is leadership."*

No matter where in the organization the vision originates, it is the leader who is its chief promoter and advocate. The *first* responsibility of the leader is to ensure that the organization is ready to accept a new vision, which, as we've seen will involve significant

"The beginning is the most important part of the work."

PLATO, (427-347 BC)
PHILOSOPHER

changes throughout the organization. Since the leader has already adjusted to the new ideas, there is sometimes a tendency to forget that others also require the opportunity to do the same. Staff need time to grow accustomed to the vision—to examine their thinking, develop a positive mindset and entertain implementation options for the new circumstances they'll be working under. Conducting group discussions and offering familiarization opportunities with others who have already moved forward might be of assistance in this process.

When the leader is satisfied that staff is indeed ready to accept the vision, it *secondly* becomes their responsibility to actively pull for the incorporation of the vision into the organization's action plan. No matter how inspiring the vision is on paper it can only become real if it is in sync with the procedures, policies and budget of the organization. No matter how inspiring the vision is on paper it can only become real when it is assessed, analyzed, adjusted on an ongoing basis.

The leader's *third* responsibility is to create a climate and a culture conducive to new ideas, to inculcating a new vision, to change. This is done by speaking about the vision enthusiastically and often; by encouraging trial and error; by celebrating successes and using failures as stepping stones; and by continuing to steadfastly believe in the vision in the face of inevitable difficulties and glitches.

Visionary leaders do not know the meaning of "can't." They don't understand obstacles or limitations. Lucille Roberts, CEO of Lucille Roberts

"Leadership is a verb, not a noun."

Health Clubs is an inspiring example. "My father lost a son in the war, and I became a surrogate son," she explains. "I never knew there was anything in the world I couldn't do. It was just a matter of when and how."

Martha Stewart is cut from the same cloth. She's up at 5:30 am to exercise and spends a dizzying day flying from TV shoots to magazine meetings to launching new "Martha" lines to supervising MarthaStewart.com. And as she puts it, "We're just getting started."

President of ClearVue Products, Brooks O'Kane's instinct is that of a visionary leader. As he comments, "a little bit of chutzpah goes a long way. Just pick up the phone and make things happen."

THE 20/20 VISION OF A LEADER

A quick look at what it takes to have 20/20 vision.

i) **Focus**
   - concentrate on key issues
   - know where to go

ii) **Affinity for others**
   - anticipate needs of others
   - communicate effectively (speak and listen)

iii) **Steadfastness**
   - maintain a clear, consistent position

iv) **Respect**
   - for self, for others
   - positive regard for self, for others

v) **Risk-taking**
   - willingness to stretch as if there were no obstacles

vi) **Self-assurance**
     - believe in the ability to make a difference

vii) **Empowerability**
     - share power
     - create opportunities for empowering oneself

viii) **Long-range vision**
     - see clearly several years down the road

ix) **Change**
     - able to encourage it
     - facilitate change in organization

x)   **Visionizing**
     - create, articulate and share visions and values

SET GOALS

Setting goals puts direction and purpose right in the middle of your vision. Without establishing specific goals, the vision lacks legs. Oprah takes a bold stand. She puts herself on the line by shouting out her goals clearly and loud-ly, then works tirelessly to accomplish them. She continuously raises her own bar. "Gut is what got me where I am today," she has often repeated.

Mary Angela Bucca set her goals quietly at Luca Industries. She was interested in advancing the causes of women and minorities at her company, but she realized she needed to begin with an issue that the organization would support. She established a local network of workers with disabilities and went on to convince managers to hold an awareness day for the group. It was not a low-key day. She brought in people to educate staff, she borrowed wheelchairs so staff could feel what working in one was like—and used sound blocks and blindfolds so that they could feel what it was like to be deaf or blind. Her awareness day made a tremendous impact. It changed things at Luca. Mary Angela had gained the confidence of managers and continued to raise awareness for the disabled. Gradually she also began raising awareness for women and minorities. With ongoing persistence and with an eye toward her goals Mary Angela achieved them, one step at a time.

To enable your vision to become reality, make a list of clear goals that you are able to control. That is, goals that are within your power to achieve—that you and your organization will work toward completing. Incrementally, these goals will help you achieve the realization of your vision. Reach your vision by setting the goals that would encourage you to work for you.

Smart Goals are Specific, Measurable and Achievable

(i) Create a Plan

> "In order to arrive at what you do not know you must go by the way which is the way of ignorance."
>
> T.S. Eliot, (1888-1965)
> Poet and critic

Share your goals with others. Together develop strategies for success. The longer-term, more complicated goals can be broken down into smaller, more easily achievable goals. At this stage it is also helpful to acknowledge the probability of obstacles and develop strategies for handling them if and when they arise.

(ii) Set Specific Goals

> "You need a plan for everything, whether it's building a cathedral or a chicken coop. Without a plan you'll postpone living until you're dead."
>
> John Goddard
> Author

Ensure that your goals are measurable. The more precise the goals, the easier it is to determine if you have achieved them. Philosophical goals are great for discussion, but poor for realization.

(iii) Set Realistic Goals

Goals should be a stretch—but attainable. Check that you have enough information, understanding, skills and knowledge to achieve the goals you've set. (If not, acquiring information and understanding would perhaps be a more realistic primary goal). Setting goals too high is discouraging, setting goals too low is counterproductive.

(iv) Specify a Timeframe

Determine not only the "what," but also the "when." Check periodically to ensure that you are on target. Discovering incongruities early in the game may give you enough time to make adjustments.

(v) Ask Goal-Setting Questions

Do this right from the start. They'll assist to keep you on track.
Ask questions such as:

- What skills are needed to achieve this goal?

- What information or knowledge is required?

- What help, collaboration or assistance is required?

- What resources are required?

- What obstacles might be encountered along the way?

- Am I making any assumptions without verification?

- Are there any alternative approaches to be considered that may be better?

- Are my goals prioritized to be effective?

Add other relevant questions and answers of your own.

INNOVATE

"Great ideas need landing
gear as well as wings."

ANONYMOUS

Keeping an enterprise going requires innovation. No one can continue to do the same thing in the same way forever. Peter F. Drucker commented that leaders are responsible for innovation; it is their duty to unrelentingly conduct or direct purposeful searches for innovation opportunities. Finding opportunities and exploiting them with effective solutions requires persistent effort.

Charlie Trotter, renown Chicago restauranteur and chef, realized innovative techniques would set him apart from other restauranteurs and persistent effort would keep him apart. From day one he insisted on using only the best ingredients. He grows some of his own herbs, has venison raised to his specifications and gets fresh fish air-freighted. He also has taken a road less traveled in his menu, which is set each night and consists of six to eight small courses. He always changes something, never serving the same menu twice. He constantly innovates and unceasingly strives for perfection. "We've received some extraordinary reviews," he says, "but you have to make sure that what you're doing remains lively and vital, and doing the same thing over and over again rarely accomplishes that."

"I must not rust."

CLARA BARTON, (1821-1912)
FOUNDER, THE AMERICAN RED CROSS

Pitney Bowes Credit Corp. (PBCC), reinvented itself as a new product powerhouse. No longer does PBCC merely finance sales and leases for existing equipment—it now creates new services. Matthew Kissner, President of Small Business and Financial Solutions wanted a fun place that would both embody their culture and convey their image.

"No straight lines, no linear thinking. Because we're a financial-services company, our biggest advantage is the quality of our ideas." PBCC's first innovation was *Purchase Power,* a revolving line of credit that helps companies finance their postage costs. Other innovations followed, inspired by an environment where people can excel—where personal performance is recognized and applauded. The hallways at PBCC encourage discussion. "We want people to bump into each other, talk about what they're doing and exchange information that they wouldn't otherwise exchange," Kissner says.

The results reflect the success of its innovative attitude. *Purchase Power* was profitable within a year of its launch and continues to grow its customer base, moreover the staff continue to be poised for new opportunities—continued innovation.

While it is possible for innovations to serendipitously appear, it is much more common for opportunity to spring either from situations within the organization or its industry—such as unexpected occurrences, incongruities, process needs or industry and market changes, or from external or environmental based developments such as demographic changes, changes in perception or new knowledge.

"A company that vigorously pursues the development of new products will actually discover opportunities as a matter of course... The CEO's chore is to judge which opportunities merit a major commitment of resources, and then determine how that market might best be served. Quite often these decisions demand that a company change the way it has been doing business."

DR. AN WANG, FOUNDER
WANG LABORATORIES , INC.

"Competition whose motive is merely to compete, to drive some other fellow out, never carries very far. The competitor to be feared is one who never bothers about you at all, but goes on making his own business better all the time. Businesses that grow by development and improvement do not die. But when a business ceases to be creative, when it believes it has reached perfection and needs to do nothing but produce—no improvement, no development—it is done."

HENRY FORD, (1863-1947), FOUNDER AND PRESIDENT
FORD MOTOR COMPANY

Consider these two examples of companies that seized opportunities for web-based innovations. The first example describes an internal based opportunity, while the second describes an external based one.

Land's End has been embroidering corporate logos on clothing for many years. Now the catalog retailer is turning its corporate sales division into an Internet operation because it feels market changes make it expedient to focus on a Business-to-Business (B2B) strategy as a growth opportunity.

The dairy industry is also embarking on a new B2B Internet exchange to sell products, initially by trading milk and cream. The venture is heralding itself as an improved way to trade a highly perishable product in an industry controlled by complex price regulations now that the technology has become available.

PRACTICE THE ABILITY TO CHANGE

> "A strong leader needs the ability to follow an ever-changing marketplace driven by technological explosions. Quick thinking, quick feet are key."
>
> DOUG RAYMOND, PRESIDENT & CEO
> RETAIL ADVERTISING AND MARKETING ASSOCIATION

In the 1960s when Alvin Toffler's *Future Shock* hit the bookshelves, it read like science fiction. The vast majority of readers were overwhelmed by the rapid acceleration of the rate of change Toffler predicted. Today not only does the change he described continue to accelerate, it does so in an ever increasing variety of forms. Leaders find themselves in the vortex of instability that change produces— yet to be effective for the long term leaders must stabilize their environments by changing in sync with the surrounding turbulence.

> "Panta rei—all is flux... (Therefore) you cannot step twice into the same river."
>
> HERACLITUS, (535-475 BC
> GREEK PHILOSOPHER

To accomplish this feat you must be prepared for change—preparation reduces anxiety tremendously and allows for a constructive response. Recognize the strategic importance of developing technological acumen. Implement a plan that involves everyone in the organization. While it is not expected that every leader will become a computer scientist, there is a distinct advantage in becoming computer literate.

It also behooves a leader in a rapidly changing environment to understand the vital role that new technology holds in today's and tomorrow's businesses; recruit, train and encourage a network of technologically astute staff; and demonstrate leadership in the understanding and use of new technology.

Implementing the plan along these lines depends on developing and maintaining an infrastructure that is both strong and flexible. It must include both the capability to transform itself—since that will inevitably be required by external pressures—yet it must maintain an integrity that remains true to its core.

Intelligent, involved human resources management and competent business units are needed to succeed. Within the organization, weave a fine and delicate thread to search for and find ideas, expertise and innovation, wherever they may reside.

> **"If we don't change,
> we don't grow.
> If we don't grow,
> we aren't really living."**
> GAIL SHEEHY
> AUTHOR

Finally expect change, expect instability. Your expectations will certainly be met. Your response will already have been considered and will be ready to implement.

The following plan offers five strategies to enable and prepare the organization to change.

> "One of a leader's most difficult challenges is assimilating information. With information exploding, the ability to assimilate the information and put it into a strategic plan is essential."
>
> PAUL PIESCHEL, SENIOR VICE PRESIDENT,
> FRANCHISE DEVELOPMENT
> MOTOPHOTO, INC.

> "Information gathering is the basis of all other managerial work, which is why I choose to spend so much of my day doing it."
>
> ANDY GROVE, CEO
> INTEL CORP.

> "A leader must be willing to take risks and learn from failures."
>
> SANDY KENNEDY, DIRECTOR,
> LEADERSHIP DIALOGUE SERIES
> ANDERSEN CONSULTING

> "Only those who will risk going too far can possibly find out how far one can go."
>
> T.S. ELIOT, (1888-1965)
> POET AND PLAYWRIGHT

(i) Be Current

Know what's happening in your field. Too obvious? Apparently not. Just recently Paco Underhill, a retail anthropologist (he tracks customer habits) spoke to a group of retailers in Toronto, Canada and asked them for feedback about a number of trend-setting international retailers. No one had a clue. How can a leader take an aggressive stand against competitors, if they don't know what is out there?

Who in the mammoth cosmetics industry, for example, was paying attention to Sephora as those involved in the organization created a global network of highly successful in-your-face retail outlets?

Scan the magazine racks. Read the dailies. Browse the Internet. Take updating courses. Get involved in clubs and associations and groups that are linked by similar interests. Meet with others in your field informally to get their take on the ever changing business picture. Attend conferences and seminars. Meet the speakers. Get the information, then discuss it with your people. Keep an eye on new developments.

Grow with your business by maintaining a strong interest in "what's new." Use all the resources at your disposal to become current and stay that way.

(ii) Be a Risk-Taker

Accept that risk is an unavoidable part of life and a certain part of business. Become a smart risk-taker by doing research, by acquiring reliable information and by soliciting expert advice. Risk is ameliorated by information.

> "We are what we think. All that we are arises with our thoughts. With our thoughts we make the world."
>
> BUDDHA, (563-483 BC)
> TEACHER, FOUNDER OF BUDDHISM

(iii) Keep Stress Under Control

Develop strategies that assist you to reduce stress and increase your well- being. Meditation, relaxation techniques, and exercise all help you to maintain good health physically and emotionally and thereby increase your flexibility to deal effectively with the challenges of today… and tomorrow.

(iv) Share Your Power

With so much information to gather in so many areas, sharing knowledge in a harmonious manner has many advantages. Leaders can no longer be expected to have all the information at their fingertips. They rely on their staffs, who are often are more knowledgeable about specific issues than they are. In our fast moving, highly technical market-

> "Telling people what to do is a thing of the past. Asking them what should be done will be the essence of leadership in the future."
>
> HEINZ FISCHER, EXECUTIVE VICE PRESIDENT, PERSONNEL DEUTSCHE-BANK AG

place, the old model of leadership just doesn't work. By asking for input and by sharing information, leaders in essence share their power and position. Shared leadership has the added benefit of allowing the cream to rise to the top. By cooperating, the person best suited to deal with an issue, a strategy, a plan is the one who deals with it. Strengths and weaknesses are balanced for the good of the organization.

(v) Develop Your Network—Grow Your Alliances

The ability to unite and manage complex alliances, partnerships and multiple networks of relationships is essential for business success. At one time partnerships were clearly delineated. Not so today. As the changing roles of customers, suppliers and partners shift and blur those lines, the critical need to forge mutually advantageous, long-term relationships with many organizations in any given industry is paramount. Ever widening connections provide fresh viewpoints and new learning approaches.

> **"Be attuned to the changing demands of an evolving market."**
>
> JOHN W. MCCONNELL, PRESIDENT & CEO
> FAIRFIELD COMMUNITIES INC.

To keep your organization propelled, not only must you change, you must get those around you to change as well. After years of observing and analyzing organizations, Peter Senge, author of *The Fifth Discipline Fieldbook: Strategies and Tools for Building a Learning Organization* and more recently *The Dance of Change: The Challenges to Sustaining Momentum in Learning Organizations*, defined leadership as, "the ability to produce change." In a May '99 interview with *Fast Company* he identified three leadership communities: *Local line leaders* are the people at the heart of the value-generating processes: those who provide services, those who design, produce and sell products. *Internal networkers* or *community builders* are the "seed carriers" who get people talking to one another. *Executive leaders* are those who focus on acting as coaches and mentors. Senge feels that in order for significant change to take place, you need to create an interplay among the three communities. Each is part of a whole entity, and each one is needed to create a positive, complete environment to produce effective on-going change.

To which leadership community do you belong?

SCENARIO PLANNING

In the early 1980s Pierre Wack of Royal Dutch/Shell wrote about scenario planning as an insightful business activity. Scenario planning, a valuable "what if?" technique is undertaken to anticipate possible future situations an organization may be required to face. Several responses are formulated to address the potential "what if?" situation, in theory, readying the organization for a future at least glimpsed at. In the late 90s, scenario planning was again advocated as a strategy that can assist organizations keep on going in uncertain times—this time by Peter Schwartz, Lawrence Wilkinson and Sean Baenen, principles of Global Business Network. At a time when the business world has become increasingly complex, when leaders are required to develop business plans in the midst of uncertainties they can't change and events they can't predict, scenario-based planning is an effective technique for recognizing and addressing possibilities and for making better decisions. By imagining future scenarios, you are able to incorporate possibilities into your strategic thinking and planning—keeping in mind that what has never been foreseen has little chance of being seen at all.

Whenever I talk about planning scenarios about the future, in my capacity as consultant, I am amazed at the light bulbs that suddenly shine bright. Imagining possibilities is empowering and energizing.

> "All that is, is a result of what we have thought."
>
> SUTTAPITAKA
> COLLECTION OF BUDDHIST WRITINGS

Begin scenario planning by considering what is going on right now in your business, your industry and around the globe. What trends have emerged? What do they impact? What *could* they impact? In addition to the business scene, what is happening politically, economically, socially and technologically? Look at *"what if?"* and *"what could?"*

> "What was once thought can never be unthought."
>
> FRIEDRICH DURRENMATT, (1921-1990)
> PLAYWRIGHT

With scenario-based planning, you are not restricted to only one possibility. (The process reminds me of the mystery books I used to buy for my kids, the ones that allowed them to choose their own ending, as many times as they wanted). Settle on a number of possibilities for the future, and for each one, develop a plan. Build contingencies into your business strategy. Incorporate measures to address future possibilities as far as is feasible.

The main point is that you have seen the future—looked it in the face and found ways to deal with it if and when it should it be necessary. This makes handling change much less frightening—much more doable.

> "My goal is to help them (his chess students) develop what I consider to be two of the most important forms of intelligence: the ability to read other people, and the ability to understand one's self. Those are the two kinds of intelligence that you need to succeed at chess—and in life."
>
> BRUCE PANDOLFINI
> CHESS MASTER, TEACHER AND AUTHOR

One final suggestion to assist you develop and maintain an ever-moving, ever-looking-for-another-solution perspective comes from the world of chess. Bruce Pandolfini, one of the most sought-after chess teachers, advocates that players never play the first good move that come into their head. He suggests that they put that move on their list of possibilities, but then ask themselves if there is an even better move. "If you see a good idea, look for a better one." In business, as in chess, good thinking is a matter of making comparisons—good, better, best—before taking action.

NURTURE A CORPORATE CULTURE

Every organization has a unique corporate culture—one that has been consciously or unconsciously developed. Successful organizations spend a great deal of energy growing and maintaining a culture that represents what they want to be and what the rest of the marketplace sees when it looks at them.

> "The moral, social and behavioral norms of an organization are based on the beliefs, attitudes and priorities of its members."
>
> AUXILLIUM WEST
> HUMAN RESOURCES SOFTWARE ORGANIZATION

Andrew Beebe, Co-founder, Chairman and CEO of Bigstep.com is very concerned with maintaining the unique corporate culture that evolved at his company from infancy. With only fifty employees, the spirit of fun and fulfillment are readily evident and permeate Bigstep's goals: to be a partner to small business, a resource to help their customers succeed. However, as the company grows Beebe realizes maintaining the corporate culture will be challenging. For the time being a well-known quote floats around the office: "Give a man a fish and he'll eat for a day. Teach a man to fish and he'll eat forever." It reinforces the vision staff at Bigstep.com have for their organization, its culture and its goals.

Unlike strategy or operations or price or product which may be imitated, a unique corporate culture is a powerful competitive advantage that is difficult to duplicate.

A pervasive corporate culture is so valuable that many of the high performance

> "I've frequently made the statement to our people: The intangibles are more important than the tangibles. Another airline can go out and get airplanes. They can acquire ticket counter space at the terminal. They can buy baggage conveyors and tags. But the hardest thing for a competitor to imitate—in the customer service business, at least—is attitude; *esprit de corps* is the way you treat customers and the way that you feel about people. And it's very difficult to emulate that, because you can't do it mechanically, and you can't do it programmatically, and you can't do it according to a formula."
>
> HERB KELLEHER, CEO
> SOUTHWEST AIRLINES

organizations align their performance goals with it. GE (General Electric), which maintains a singleness of purpose from top to bottom, provides an excellent example. Everything within the company—every strategy, every program, every measure—supports its goals. There are no mixed messages, no crossed signals. All the way from Jack Welch's vision down the line to the daily performance of frontline staff, none of the cohesive purpose is lost.

Talk to a GE Manager and you can almost hear Jack Welch echoing the words. While less focused organizations may have effective strategies, well designed processes, as well as capable and well-intentioned staff, without a powerful, tightly integrated culture that motivates internal synergy, the best of efforts are not translated into positive results. Instead of a powerful and seamless corporate stance, there is fragmentation, misalignment, lack of focus and finally mediocrity.

Effective performance measurement begins by setting goals that speak to the core of the organization. The core being defined as that which is truly important to the organization, as evidenced by everyone's behavior every day.

A study of excellently managed companies, including IBM, P & G (Procter & Gamble) and McDonald's found that corporate culture consists of four elements. The first element is style of behavior and thinking. For example, at Wal-Mart there is a greeter who welcomes customers in the traditional Wal-Mart way—friendly and down-to-earth.

The second element is skills. Employees at these and other exemplary organizations have mastered the skills necessary to implement their business strategy. Retailers like JCPenney, Wal-Mart and Wachovia Bank have used the infrastructures they have in place, including the skills of their trained staff, to implement *their* business strategy—selling on-line from selling on the floor.

The third element is staffing—hiring the right people for the right job and then training them to be even better. Herb Kelleher relates how a Vice President in Amarillo, Texas apologized for interviewing 34 people for a ramp agent position and still had not hiring anyone. Kelleher replied, "If you have to interview 134 people to get the right attitude… do it."

The fourth element is shared values. Everyone in the organization from top to bottom needs to believe in the same guiding values and mission— and to be proud to practice them. If the number of applicants per job opening is any indication, companies such as Southwest Airlines, Wal-Mart stores, Cisco Systems and GE (General Electric) maintain corporate cultures which attract a huge number of people. Each has made it to the Top Ten of *Fortune*'s 100 Best Companies to Work For in 2000.

When all these elements are present in an organization, the corporate culture becomes a powerful, unique factor. The corporate culture of a company is a facet of that company's over-arching vision, it's guiding philosophy. Establishing a strong vision and philosophy—one that everyone from the CEO on down subscribes to—requires some effort, especially since organizations are comprised of individuals with competing beliefs and unique "I" perspectives.

Consider some suggestions for enhancing corporate culture in the face of conflicting individual interests. One useful idea is to hold an off-site meeting—a weekend retreat would be great—where the group can come together as a team. Give employees the opportunity to express themselves and to discuss where they would like to see the organization next year, in five years, in ten years. By arriving at a consensus the group grows closer together. Ask for their input on the strengths and weaknesses they see within the organization and for their recommendations for improvement.

Danette Mueller, of Leverage Systems in St. Paul suggests garnering participation by making it clear that you value the business experience of staff. In this way she says, "people will be less likely to sabotage progress and more likely to work together." Strive to get everyone to believe in the process—you need your employees to help build your vision. Without their support your vision remains only a framed axiom on the wall.

Develop a step-by-step plan to grow the culture that you envision. Monitor the results. Make note of whether the anticipated corporate culture is being nurtured or if the organization is going off on some unforeseen, undesirable direction. For example, if one of the goals is to create an environment that emphasizes workers' family needs, does the required daycare exist—is it being well utilized? Is it an example for other organizations to follow? If one of the goals of your prospective culture is to encourage feedback from everyone, are there mechanisms in place that facilitate giving feedback, encouraging suggestions and ideas?

> "Tell me, I'll forget. Show me, I may remember. But involve me and I'll understand."
>
> CHINESE PROVERB

The rewards for a cohesive corporate culture are so substantial in terms of employee retention and productivity, improved customer service, greater organizational stability, and larger profits that a leader can ill afford to ignore them.

EXECUTION IS THE STRATEGY

Every leader I spoke with agreed that execution is essential, since without consistent action, ideas remain only wishful thinking, plans remain only hopeful schemes. Execution is so essential to today's marketplace leaders that it in fact, becomes a strategy of its own.

Great leaders recognize that "getting it done" is absolutely necessary, but they also realize it cannot be their task alone. A leader must certainly execute, but at the same time they must enable everyone around them to assist, to be involved.

"Example is not the main thing in infuencing others...it is the only thing."

DR. ALBERT SCHWEITZER, (1875-1965)
PHILOSOPHER AND PHYSICIAN

At the end of many of the programs I conduct, I reiterate that a leader's responsibility is to instill execution-fever in their people. As far as I'm concerned the three most important things a leader can do is:

a) **Be an example.**

b) **Be an example.**

c) **Be an example.**

"A leader is one who can lay out a road map with a specific goal that creates success for the organization and all employees in a manner that is forceful but not threatening."

MARK TOWE, PRESIDENT & CEO
OLDCASTLE MATERIALS, INC.

Max DePree ends his book *Leadership is an Art* with a comment that all leaders must take to heart, head and hand, "The visible signs of artful leadership are expressed, ultimately, in its practice."

"I cannot tell you how many great ideas that I have had, that I have seen other individuals or companies bring to fruition. True leaders have the conviction, determination and passion to take action on their ideas." Ross Lederer of Craft-Bilt Manufacturing Co, concurs eloquently with this statement.

A leader must lead. From two very different quarters come strikingly similar observations. Orit Gadiesch, Chairman of Bain & Co., a management consulting firm, did a stint in the Israeli army. She talked to *Forbes ASAP* about her observations. "I saw a lot of leaders there… in the Israeli army, the officers are out in front and say 'Follow me,' whereas in most military settings the officers yell, 'charge!' That is the one reason the Israeli army has been so successful. I'm seeing more leaders now willing to say 'follow me.' "

Peter Drucker arrived at the same conclusion. He related in a column he wrote that when he was in high school his history teacher, a badly wounded war veteran, asked the class to review selected World War I books. During the discussions one of Drucker's classmates commented, "Every one of those books say that the Great War was a war of total military incompetence. Why was it?" The teacher didn't hesitate, but shot right back, "Because not enough generals were killed; they stayed way behind the lines and let others do the fighting and dying."

> "One of a leader's greatest challenges is to keep the organization focused, ensuring that everyone receives the same message and acts in a coordinated fashion."
>
> LARRY QUINLIVAN, VICE PRESIDENT, MARKETING
> NATIONAL STONE ASSOCIATION

Execution makes you a better planner, thinker, player, leader. It makes your people better employees, and your customers happier. Execution is anti-stagnant. It keeps things fresh, clean, moving.

The process of keeping an organization vibrant, alive and forward focused remains the same for everyone—only the specific details of implementation change with the changing face of the organization.

Would you work for you?   Yes ☐ No ☐ I'm not sure at this time ☐

SOME TOUGH QUESTIONS

1. What does your vision of the future look like?
    What do you see a year down the road? Five years down the road?

    _____

    _____

    _____

2. What steps are you taking to communicate your vision to those around you
    and to make them part of your vision?

    _____

    _____

    _____

3. What steps are you taking to make your vision a reality?
    What goals are you setting? How are you involving your people in your task?

    _____

    _____

    _____

4. What goal setting questions besides the ones in this chapter do you
    need to ask and answer in regard to your organization?

    _____

    _____

    _____

5. Where do you look for new opportunities?
   What innovations have you instituted in the last year?

   _____

   _____

   _____

6. How prepared are you for the inevitability of change? How prepared are your
   people? What else can you do to increase your preparedness?

   _____

   _____

   _____

7. Have you ever attempted scenario planning? What did you discover?
   What did you do with the options you developed?

   _____

   _____

   _____

8. How would you describe your corporate culture? How cohesive is it?

   _____

   _____

   _____

9. What can you do to strengthen and enhance your corporate culture?
   How can you elicit assistance from your people in this task?

   _____

   _____

   _____

10. Why would or wouldn't you work for you, based on your ability to keep
    the organization going?

    _____

    _____

    _____

    _____

Chapter 7

Summary - Leaders As Human Beings

Would You Work for You?
*Yes, if Only... **You Know How to "Be"***

When Marshall McLuhan talked about a global village in the 1960s, I don't think anyone ever imagined it would look like this. Today's global village demands of its leaders capabilities, intuition and mental agility not previously expected or required. Not only do leaders need to know, they need to know *what to know*—not only how to access information but how to access *the most relevant information* and separate it from the chaff.

> "Fit no stereotypes. Don't chase the latest management fads. The situation dictates which approach best accomplishes the team's mission."
>
> General Colin Powell,
> Chairman (Retired), Joint Chiefs of Staff

Today's leaders must function successfully in both a global and local environment. Their bifocals must be perfectly tempered so they can see the big global picture as well as the local details. They must demonstrate a personal mastery over themselves, their organizations and their people. Yet they must be the first to realize they can't be "super heroes." They must surround themselves with exceptional groups of professionals—experts in areas where they lack expertise—so the combined strength of the team outperforms any one of the players.

Today's leaders must squeeze the most value from every situation. They must think in terms of creating value through their people, their processes and their technology. Doing business globally requires the ability to find the means to extract more value on an international scale.

Today's leaders never forget the two faces of time—fast and faster. There is no slow—move your organization ahead of the competition. Shave a few seconds off completing a transaction or developing a product or a process and your efficiency reverberates.

Today's leaders live with a new sense of space—a borderless world. Distance has vanished. Connectivity knows no boundaries—customers are everywhere, so are competitors. Global leaders live in a communication-intensive environment, where phone, fax, e-mail, web, intranet and face-to-face interactions are all part of the normal business day. The hi-tech world has kissed the leader with high-communication opportunities.

Finally, today's leaders live among their crown jewels—their human cargo of brainpower. In a knowledge-based economy the emphasis is on the people who come up with the smart ideas, the innovative technologies, and the better business models. They have become invaluable—they know it, you know it. It is the leader's role to develop human capital, ensuring an environment that stimulates workers, that facilitates effective collaboration, that refreshes and renews. Leaders must always be reinventing their knowledge base—creating a strong network

> "No matter how big the fast food retailing giant becomes, we have to remember that the job is done by individual human beings."
>
> Jim Kuhn, Vice President, Individuality McDonalds Corporation

that encourages the human capital, their employees to use their intelligence, knowledge and creativity to help precipitate break-throughs in their industry. Leaders must surround themselves with people whose motivations, perspectives, and thought processes are similar to theirs, yet whose strengths are different from theirs, so that a balance is created and maintained.

David W. Hockenbrocht, President of Sparton Corp. in Jackson, MI, summed up the global leader's role very effectively, "in a very real way, a CEO today is responsible for the leadership of the mind and the practice of the business." Not an easy task!

After coming to grips with everything we must know as leaders, we find there is still more to do. We must look at ourselves in the mirror every morning, see in that reflection who we want to become and work all day toward that learning, growing and becoming.

We are not complete. Each experience changes us in some measure. Our values—those assumptions and beliefs we hold about what is good or bad, what is desirable or unde-sirable, what is important or unimportant—influence our thought processes, our decisions, our actions.

"Trust men, and they will be true to you. Treat them greatly, and they will show themselves great."

RALPH WALDO EMERSON, (1803-1882)
AUTHOR AND POET

"Your thoughts become your words. Your words become your actions. Your actions become your habits. Your habits become your character... so your character comes out of your thoughts."

ANONYMOUS

"It doesn't happen all at once... you become. It takes a long time."

MARGERY WILLIAMS, (1880-1944)
AUTHOR

Outstanding leaders must maintain personal values that conform with societal demands, expectations and norms. In today's society that translates into leaders who are humane, authentic individuals who have integrity, who have rooted values and live by them.

> "We get through to people to the extent that we have unconditional regard for them as human beings."
>
> Carl Rodgers
> Industrialist

Becoming an authentic person involves understanding not only what actions to take, but also appreciating how those actions affect others. Great leaders exemplify behavior that not only leads to self-fulfillment, but also demonstrates a concern for and commitment to others.

The challenge does not end there since leaders of today will inevitably be involved in tomorrow's organizations. It is within this context that exemplary leaders continue to search for viable solutions to change what must be changed, but remain ever cognizant to preserve essential, valid values.

Becoming the leader that you and others would want to work for is an exciting, stressful, overwhelming, never-ending quest. As you continue that quest, carry with you both the lantern and the shovel. Hold the lantern high and you will also see the possibilities all around you. Dig the shovel deep and you will unearth the opportunities that are to be found only by persistent effort.

Be a leader's leader. Listen. Learn. Lead. Live. Laugh.

ADDITIONAL RESOURCES

As a professional speaker, Sam Geist delivers customized keynotes, conducts workshops and seminar presentations as well as consults and facilitates for many of North America's foremost organizations and associations. The programs focus on a variety of business-oriented topics including: business management and strategy, leadership, differentiation, the changing marketplace, customer service and motivating staff.

Would You Work for You? and **Why Should Someone Do Business With You... Rather Than Someone Else?** are available in bookstores across North America.

Audio and video tapes are available for these and other programs

Addington & Wentworth offers corporate rates on orders of ten or more books.

To inquire about ordering books in volume please call 1-800-567-1861 or email us at samgeist@geistgroup.com

In conjunction with this book, Sam has developed a new seminar presentation, appropriately entitled, *Would You Work for You?* When presenting this program he includes information from the book as well as from other relevant sources.

To inquire about this program or any one of Sam Geist's other presentations please call 1-800-567-1861 or email us at samgeist@geistgroup.com

Visit Sam's website for additional program and resource information at http://www.samgeist.com

INDEX